Sketch Pedigrees

of some of the

Early Settlers in Jamaica

Noël B. Livingston

CLEARFIELD COMPANY

Originally Published
Jamaica, 1909

Reprinted for
Clearfield Company, Inc. by
Genealogical Publishing Company Inc.
Baltimore, Maryland
1992

ISBN 0-8063-5072-5

—TO—
SIR FIELDING CLARKE

CHIEF JUSTICE OF JAMAICA & KEEPER OF THE RECORDS.

This Volume is, by his kind permission, dedicated.

CONTENTS.

PART I. Sketch Pedigrees.

PART II. A proclamation for the Encouraging of Planters in His Majesty's Island of Jamaica.

PART III. A short account of Jamaica when Sir Charles Littleton left it in 1664.

PART IV. Propositions for the Speedy Settling of Jamaica.

PART V. A List of the Trained Bands taken in June 1670.

PART VI. A List of the Ships under the Command of Admiral Morgan.

PART VII. Report by Sir Thomas Modyford to Lord Arlington in 1670.

PART VIII. Survey (List of Inhabitants) 1670.

PART IX. Pedigree of Robert Hunter, Governor of Jamaica.

INTRODUCTORY NOTE.

The records of the Court of Chancery of this Island yielding, as they do, a vast amount of interesting information chiefly genealogical, have hitherto been an entirely neglected field of research in Jamaica—this is a matter greatly to be deplored for what with want of care, the accumulated dust of years, damp, mildew and moths they are quickly going to complete destruction, and it is for the purpose of preserving some of the material obtained therefrom that I have decided to publish these sketch pedigrees.

I regret that my reference cannot be more accurate by giving the liber and folio at which the proceedings from which the compiled pedigrees are recorded but the volumes lack in most cases both covers and index, in fact many of the volumes that do boast covers lack information, moths having already been at their work of destruction by eating away the pages!

The other old records of the Island consisting of Patents of land and of Deeds, the records of the now obsolete Court of Ordinary (consisting of Wills, Letters of Administration and Inventories) and the registers of births, marriages and deaths for the various Parishes have been carefully preserved and are in excellent order and condition, and perhaps the following table shewing when the dates of these registers for the various Parishes commence may be of interest.

Parish	Baptisms.	Marriages.	Burials.
Kingston	1722	1721	1722
Port Royal	1728	1727	1725
St. Andrew	1664	1668	1666
St. Thos ye East	1709	1721	1708
St. David	1794	1794	1794
Portland	1804	1804	1808
St. George	1806	1807	1811
St. Mary	1752	1755	1767
Clarendon	1690	1695	1769
St. Ann	1768	1768	1768
Manchester	1816	1827	1817
St. Catherine	1668	1668	1671
St. John	1751	1751	1751
St. Dorothy	1693	1725	1706
St. Thos ye Vale	1816	1816	1816
Metcalfe	1843	1843	1843

Parish.	Baptisms.	Marriages.	Burials.
Westmoreland	1740	1740	1741
St. Elizabeth	1708	1719	1720
Trelawney	1771	1771	1771
St. James	1770	1772	1774
Vere	1696	1743	1733
Hanover	1725	1754	1727

In conclusion I beg to thank all those who have so kindly come forward in response to my circular and trust that they will each find something to specially interest them in the following pages.

NOËL B. LIVINGSTON.

Kingston, Jamaica.

PART I.

SKETCH PEDIGREES.

NOTE.—Names in brackets ( ) in the following pedigrees were not obtained from the records but from other sources of information.

ALLEN vs. PENNINGTON.

Bill filed 14th August 1764.

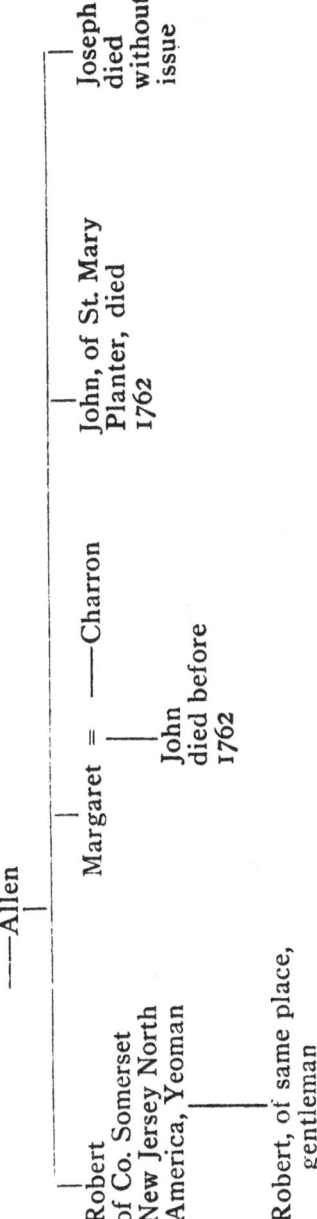

```
                    ——Allen
         ┌─────────────┴─────────────┐
         |                  Margaret = ——Charron
         |                       ┌───────┴───────┐
         |                       |               |
         |                      John    John, of St. Mary   Joseph
         |                   died before  Planter, died     died
         |                      1762         1762          without
         |                                                  issue
  ┌──────┴──────┐
  Robert        Robert, of same place,
  of Co. Somerset  gentleman
  New Jersey North
  America, Yeoman
```

ARMSTRONG ET UX VS. GORDON ET AL.

Bill filed 28 November 1764

```
       Henry Bonner━━━━Catherine
    of St. Dorothy Esq.   d. intestate
       D. 22 March 1729   21 July 1730
                   │
              John = Rebecca ━━━━ 3rdly Martin Armstrong
                     widow of Richard      of Kingston Merchant
                     Corr of Kingston
                     gentleman.
```

Bonner—Henry was a Member of the Assembly for St. Ann 1722.

See also Russell vs. Bonner.

ASHLEY vs. DAWKINS (Exor.) ET AL.

Bill filed 1st October 1764.

```
                    Thomas Rule
                    of Clarendon, Planter
                    Will d/d 13th Feb. 1734.
        ┌───────────────────────┴───────────────────────┐
                                              Thomas      = Elizabeth Joanna ......
                                              21 in 1752    died prior to
                                              Will d/d 22   1762.
                                              Sept. 1762
Thomas Ashley = 2nd Elizabeth = 1st George Buchanan
of Clarendon      16 in 1749    of Clarendon planter
Planter                         died 1747 intestate
M. 1750                         M. 1745
                        ┌───────────┴───────────┐
                       Ann              Thomas Rule,
```

NOTE.—There was a James Rule who was a Member of the Assembly for Vere 1719–1722 and for Clarendon 1711, 1716, 1718 and 1722 who was most probably the Father of Thomas.

Rules Pen in Clarendon and Ashley in the same Parish still bear the old settlers' names.

AUDLEY vs. O'BRIEN.

Final Decree filed in 1775.

```
Thomas Audley  =  Martha          ────Russell
of Kingston,      m. 1771        │            │
Cordwainer                    Frances  =  1st Thomas Parker, of Kingston,
                              d. 24         Mariner, d. 29th Feb. 1752.
                              Jan. 1769
                                       =  2ndly William Fay, Merchant
                                           m. 24th March 1753, died 1760.
                                           │
                                        Mary Elizabeth Crean Fay.
```

AYLMER vs. AYLMER.

Bill filed 16th September 1719.

HALSTEAD vs. BROWN.

Bill filed 18th November 1762

```
                              Whitgift Aylmer = (Joyce)
                               of St. John, Esq.
      ┌──────────────┬──────────────┬──────────────┬──────────────┐
Stephen Browne 2nd = Gertrude = 1st Whitgift   Samuel      Judith = —Bathurst   Mary      Catharine
m. 1729                         of St. John    of St. John of Saint             of St.    of St.
                                Esq., d. 20    Planter     Catherine            Catherine Catherine
                                Augt. 1720                 widow in 1719

                    Catherine = Honble John Burke, Esq.
                                of Jamaica, and in 1762
                                Lord Viscount Mayo of
                                Kingdom of Ireland.
```

NOTES.—Whitgift Aylmer was Member of the Assembly for St. John 1674 1677, and 1701 for St. Ann 1679 1688 Assistant Judge of Common Pleas St. John 1675.

The following inscriptions from the Church of St. Johns Parish are from Lawrence Archers Monumental Inscriptions "Here lies the body of the Honble. Col. Whitgift Aylmer who after he had lived in this Island 46 yrs 2 m 10 d deptd. this life 20 July being Sunday 1707 aet 67 yrs 4 m 3 d."

ARMS. A cross between 4 birds close.

"Here lies the body of Madame Joyce Aylmer the wife of the Honble. Col. Whitgift Aylmer who dep. this life 18 Sep. 1702 aet 52 years."

Whitgift Aylmer junior was Member of the Assembly St. James 1701, Port Royal 1704, St. John 1702, 1706-9. Saint Catherine 1715, St. George 1716, St. Davids 1718.

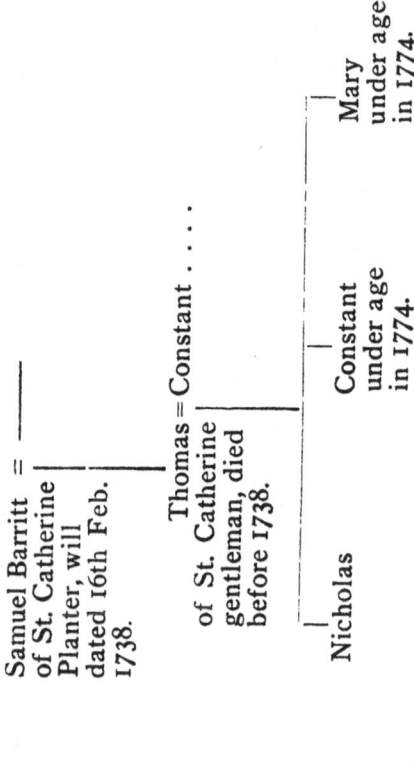

BASNETT vs. GARTHWAITE.

Bill filed 19th February 1739.

```
         Edward Cook    =   Mary ─────┐
        of St. James Esq.             │
         died 8th Aug. 1719.          │
    ┌────────┴────────┐               │
Richard Basnett = Mary    Thomas      Edward
of St. Mary, Esquire.   died aged 2.  died 7th Jan. 1735.
```

NOTE.—Edward Cook was Member of the Assembly for St. Marys Parish 1711.

BLAKE vs. CROWDEN.

Bill filed 12th Novr. 1776.

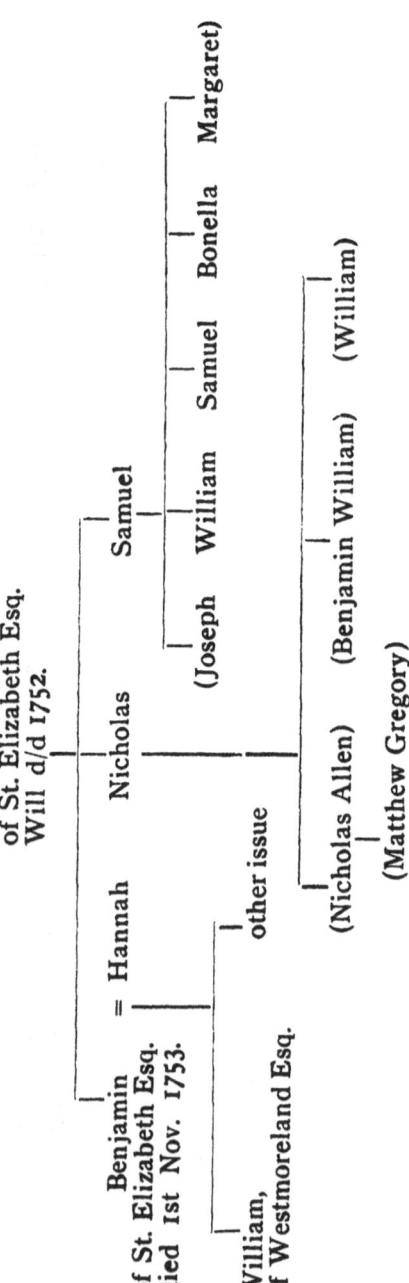

BOOTH vs. BOOTH.

Bill filed 2nd July 1766.

SAMUEL BOOTH = Mary = 2ndly George Booth
of Vere, Esq.,   of Vere, Esq.
died 1760.

Simon   Thomas Harcy Barritt = Eleanor.

NOTE.—George Booth was a Member of the Assembly for the Parish of Vere 1745, 1749, 1759, 1761.

Thomas Harcy Barritt was also a Member for the same Parish 1773 and a Member of the Council 1775.

BOSLEY vs. WHEATLE.

Bill filed 5th July 1766.

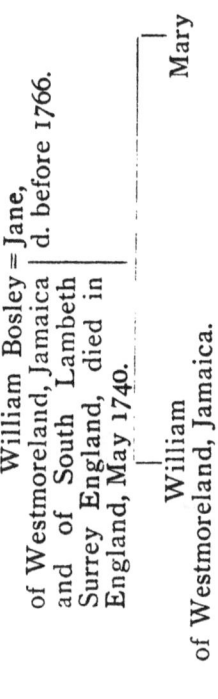

William Bosley = Jane,
of Westmoreland, Jamaica | d. before 1766.
and of South Lambeth
Surrey England, died in
England, May 1740.

William — Mary
of Westmoreland, Jamaica.

BURKE vs. HALL.

Bill filed 29th August 1775.

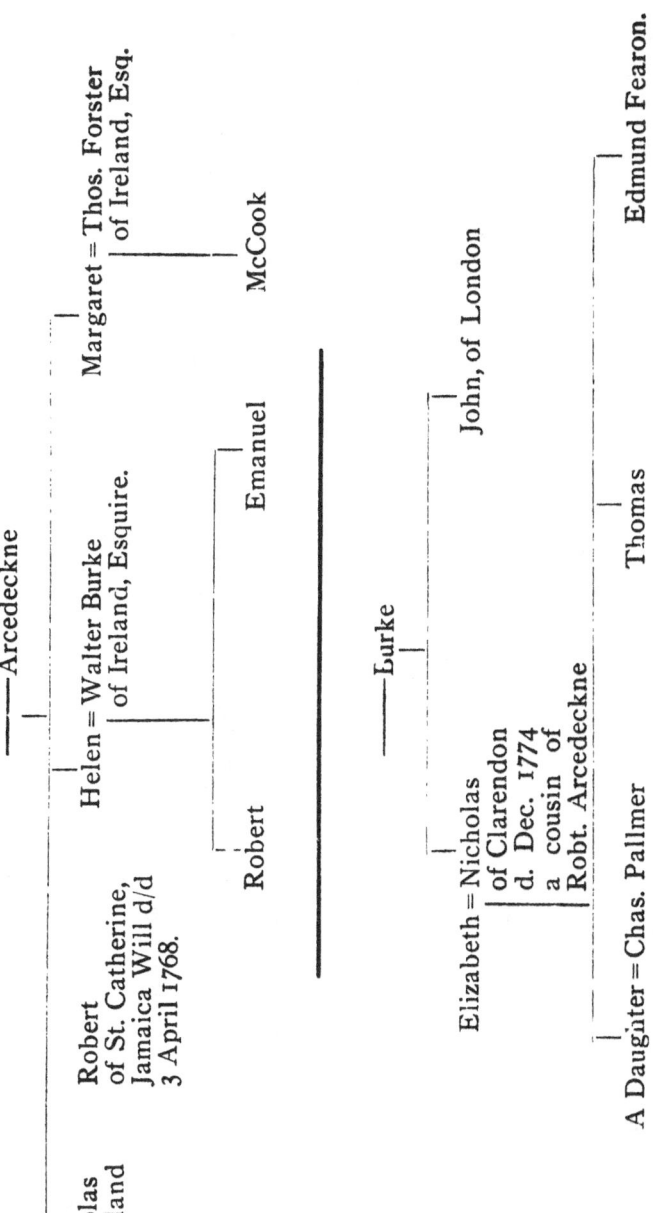

BYNDLOSS vs. MARTINS.

Petition filed 19th April 1772.

```
                              ┌─────────── Byndloss ───────────┐
                              │                                │
Robert                     Henry Morgan                    Matthew                Thomas.
of St. Thomas in the Vale, died 1757.                     died Sept. 1765
Esquire, died Dec. 1753.
        │                      │
   ┌────┴────┐                  │
Matthew    Susanna  =  Archibald Sympson      Ann Masters         Frances
of St. Catherine  married  of Vere Prac; in Physic  of Great Britain    of St. Catherine.
gentleman.  Feb. 1769    and Surgery.              Spinster
            d. Nov. 1769
```

Byndloss Robert was Member of the Assembly, St. Catherine 1744.

Byndloss Henry Morgan, Member of the Assembly, St. Mary 1754 and 1755, Attorney General 1754.

Simpson, Archibald, Member of the Assembly, Vere 1775, 1787, 1790.

CHOVETT vs. ARCEDECKNE.

Bill filed 13th July 1765.

```
Henry Long  (Nathaniel Grey) = (Dorothy Wood)
                    |
        Priscilla = (Major Samuel) Guy
        died 1748   (bapt. 16 Nov. 1681
        of St. Andrew. m. 6 Dec. 1704.)
              |
              |——————————————————|
                                  |
                          1st————Maverly
                                  |
                          Elizabeth = Organ Furnell
                                      of Jamaica
                                      and Great Britain
                                      Mariner.

Abraham Chovett    2nd = Martha
of St. Catherine, Esq.   d. 4 Sept.
                         1762.
```

CRICHTON vs. HALL.

Answer filed 26th July 1766.

```
                    ———Philp———
                    |                        |
                 Mathias              Margaret = Francis East
              Will d/d Dec. 1745.         |
                                          |
                          Edward Rookwood = Martha        East, of Kingston
                          of St. Andrew, planter.              Spinster.
                                          |
                                    Frances
                                  of Kingston,
                                    Spinster.

Elizabeth = Robert Crichton
           of Kingston, Gentleman
```

Francis East in 1716 was Member of the Assembly for St. Andrew.

CROASDALE vs. BAYLEY.

Bill filed 28th July 1769.

Hargreaves = Elizabeth = 2nd Joseph Etough
of Kingston, Merchant.

Mary = Henry Croasdale
of Kingston, Esq.

Suasannah = ——Jowett
Cavalier.

CONNOR vs. BROOKS.

Bill filed 14th May 1764.

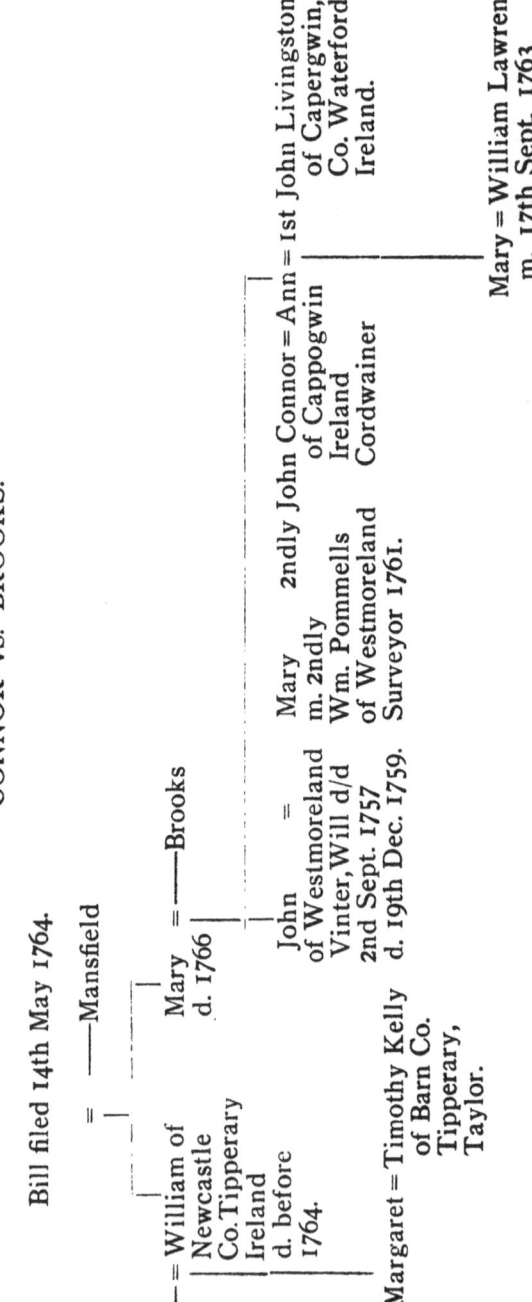

――― = ――――Mansfield
        |
   ―――――――――――
   | |
= William of   Mary = ―――Brooks
  Newcastle   d. 1766
  Co. Tipperary
  Ireland
  d. before
  1764.
        |
   ―――――――――――
   | |
   John   =   Mary   2ndly John Connor = Ann = 1st John Livingston
   of Westmoreland m. 2ndly   of Cappogwin   of Capergwin,
   Vinter, Will d/d Wm. Pommells Ireland   Co. Waterford
   2nd Sept. 1757   of Westmoreland Cordwainer   Ireland.
   d. 19th Dec. 1759. Surveyor 1761.
        | |
Margaret = Timothy Kelly   Mary = William Lawrence
           of Barn Co.   m. 17th Sept. 1763
           Tipperary,   corporal in H.M.
           Taylor.   13th Regt. of Green
                                                   Dragons.

DAWKINS vs. YOUNG.

Bill filed 29th July 1710.

Richard Dawkins = Elizabeth = 2nd Valentine Mumbee
of Clarendon Esq. | d. Dec. 1708.   of Vere Esq.
Will dated 1698.

Richard

NOTE.—Richard Dawkins was Member of the Assembly, Clarendon, 1679, 1688, 1693.

DOUGLAS vs. DAWES.

Bill filed 14th August 1765.

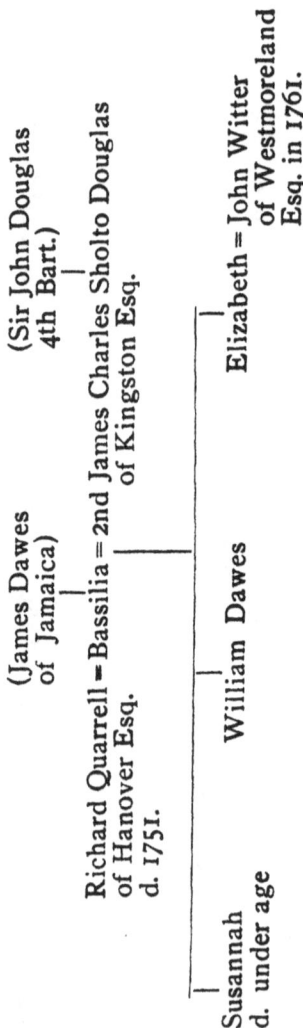

NOTE.—James Charles Sholto Douglas was Collector of Customs for Jamaica circa 1760.

Quarrell Richard was member of the Assembly for Hanover 1749.

Quarrell, William Dawes was in 1799 a Commissioner for Forts and Fortifications.

Dawes James, Member of the Assembly 1755-6, 1761.

DOWLEN vs. FREEMAN.

Bill filed 26th July, 1710.

Thomas Freeman
of St. Thomas the Apostle
d. 1st Sept. 1690.

```
        |                                           |
Modyford = Grace = 2nd Hugh Totterdell    Thomas    Elizabeth = Joseph Dowlen
          d. 9 Jany. 1698.                                         of St. Thomas
                                                    |
                                       (Richard Guy) = 2nd (Mary Davenport)
                                                     | m. 12th Feb. 1674.
                                                     |
                                              (Mary) = (Richard Lloyd)
                                                  m. 24th July
                                                      1690.
                                      John = (Katherine)
                                   of St. John   2nd daughter.
```

FREEMAN JOHN, Member of the Assembly, St. John, 1694-5, 1701-1704.
TOTTERDELL HUGH, Member of the Assembly, St. Catherine, 1701, 1704, 1707, 1714, St. George, 1703. Port Royal 1706, St. David 1709, Kingston 1711, Speaker of the House in 1706 and 1714.
GUY, RICHARD was Member of the Assembly, Northside 1671, St. Ann 1673, St. James 1675, 1677, 1679 He lies buried in the old Parish Church of St. John.
"Here lyeth buryed the body of Richard Guy, Esq., who dyed the 10th day of June 1681, aged 63 years. He had by his beloved wife 4 children. Mary the eldest, Richard and Katherine twins and Susanna the youngest. Richard dyed young and lyes buryed in this grave. Susanna also dyed young in England whither she was sent to be educated and lies buried in Hackney Church near London." (Lawrence Archer).

DOWNER vs. REID.

Bill filed 29th November 1710.

Arthur Goodwin
of Vere Planter
Will 18th April 1693.

```
        |────────────────────────────────|
                                      Arthur
|───────────|───────────|
Grace    Mary      Judith = John Downer
        died early  married   of Vere Planter
                   Sept. 1707  under age
                               in 1710
```

Thomas = Sarah = 2nd William Reid
married   of Vere Esq.
11th Aug.
1700.

DRAX vs. BRAYNE.

Bill filed 9th December 1710.

William Drax = Mary = 2nd = Thomas Brayne
in July 1689   died   of St. Ann them of
left Jamaica   15 Nov.   St. Catherine, gent.
               1709   married 18 Augt. 1698.

Charles
of St. Ann Planter.

William Drax was Member of the Assembly for St. Ann 1686.

Charles Drax was Member of the Assembly, St. Ann 1702, St. David 1707, St. Mary 1708, St. George 1710–1, St. James 1719.

Thomas Brayne was Member of the Assembly for St. Ann 1702–3.

32

FORD vs. MITCHELL.

Bill filed 5th Sept. 1770.

```
                                    ┌──────────────Ford
                                    │
        ┌──────┬─────────┬──────────┼──────────┐
     Gilbert  John   Edward = Elizabeth   Thomas      James
   of St. Catherine  d. before                    of Albemarle St.
     d. Oct. 1767.     1767                       Piccadilly, England
                                                   Dr. of Physic.
                        │                              ║
                    Elizabeth                 ┌────────┴────────┐
                                          Anna Maria        Gilbert
```

Gilbert Ford was Attorney General 1760 and Member of the Assembly for St. John 1761, Member of the Council 1764.

```
                    ┌──────────Ayscough
                    │
            ┌───────┴───────┐
          John         Thomas = Mary
                      of St. Catherine
                         d. 1755
                              │
                    Grace Harrison = David Robert Mitchell
                         m. 1764        of Great Britain.
```

FREEMAN vs. BENNETT.

Bill filed 31st July 1710.

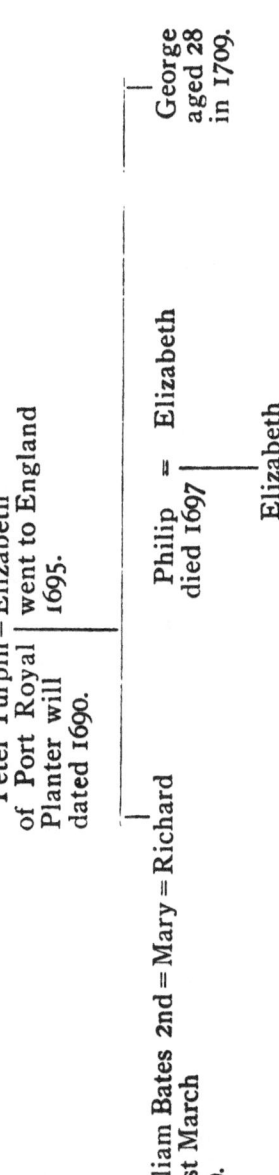

Peter Turpin = Elizabeth
of Port Royal went to England
Planter will 1695.
dated 1690.

William Bates 2nd = Mary = Richard   Philip = Elizabeth
d. 1st March
1709.
                                          died 1697

Elizabeth   George
                aged 28
                in 1709.

GARDNER vs. BECKFORD.

Bill filed 9th October 1742.

```
John Gardner =
of St. Catherine, Esq.,
died 1722.
         |
    ┌────┴────┐
  John =      Thomas = Ann
  died 1734
    |
  ┌─┴──────────┐
  John       2 daughters
  of Clarendon, Esq.
  aged 12 in 1734.
```

John Gardner the elder represented St. John in the House of Assembly 1718, Clarendon 1719, 1721–2.

FREEMAN vs. PUTMAN or PUTNAM.

Bill filed 30th September 1678.

Thomas Johnson
of Morant, St. Thomas, Esq.,
Will dated 20th April 1677.

```
              |-----------------------------|
    |-------------------|                   |
   Mary  =  John Putman (or Putnam)        Ann         Elizabeth
married   of Morant, a relative of                     d. 1677/1678.
March 1678 Thomas Freeman who was
           Executor of Thomas Johnson.
```

GILLESPIE vs. HUME.

Bill filed 21st July 1772.

```
                        Lucock Griffin =
                        died 1749.
                               |
              ┌────────────────┴────────────────┐
        Giles John = Mary Henrietta
              |
    ┌─────────┬──────────────┬──────────────┐
  Mary   Elizabeth    Lucock = Mary Amelia   John Poppleton   Samuel Brocklesby
         b. 17th      2nd John Gillespie     b. 14th Novr.    born 24th Jan. 1758.
         July 1751.   of Kingston            1754.
                      gentleman.
                      daughter of
                      Augustin Merida
                      aged 20 in 1772.
```

In the Kingston Parish Churchyard is a tombstone to the memory of Mary the wife of Lucock Griffin of Kingston, Carpenter, who died the 17th October 1741 aged 49 years.

Lucock Griffin was Member of the Assembly for Kingston 1745-1749.

GORDON vs. CARGILL.

Bill filed 1775.

──Barclay = Ann
            │
          ──Gordon──
            │   │
    ┌───────┬──────────┬────────┬──────────┬──────────┬─────────┬──────────┬──────────┐
  James, George=Mary Jean=Thomas Susannah Elizabeth Mary Jean Charles James John
  of St. died   of d. prior married   all of Aberdeen.   late of of   of
  Andrew before   Aber- to 1775 John   King-   King- Edin-
  Esq. inter- 1765.   deen. Merchant Gordon   ston,   ston, burgh,
  ested in lands   of Aber- of Crichie   Jamaica Mer-   Esq.
  Cairinglass   deen.   Aberdeen   Merchant, chant.
  Cairnies and   (also called   d. July
  Invernoth in   Ann.)   1775.
  Aberdeen late
  part of estate
  of Lord Salton
  decd. died Jan.
  1765. Refers in
  will to his Bro-
  thers in law
  Capt. John
  Thompson and
  John Gordon of
  Edinburgh, Advocate.

                    │   │
         Ann, = William Young of   Jean, 21 on
         21 on 3rd June Aberdeen, Dr. of   1st May 1768.
         1766.   Physick.

                                                              │
                                              Charles of Kingston
                                              late of Aberdeen
                                              21 on 28th March 1770.

37

GORDON vs. MACKAY.

Bill filed 3rd December 1763.

```
                    ————MacKay         Sinclair
                          |                |
         ┌────────────────┴────────┐       |
         |                         |       |
    Hugh                      Hugh MacKay = 1st Sarah Morgan = 2nd Dr. John Gordon
    of St. Ann, Esq.          Lieut. in H.M.                      of St. Mary.
    married Mother            74th Regt. of
    of Dr. John               Foot, d. Aug. 14
    Gordon.                   1762, no issue.
```

GRACE vs. CLARKE.

Bill filed 1775.

```
                    John Clarke =
                    of St. Davids, Esq.,
                    Will d/d 28 June 1720.
        ┌───────────────────────┼───────────────┬───────────────────────┐
2ndly Richard Grace=Mary──=Edward of St. Davids,    Sarah      Elizabeth =J. Calendar
of St. Davids, planter                                        =2ndly Sir Archibald
(complainants.)                                                Grant of London.
```

John Clarke was Member of the Assembly for St. David 1693, 1698, 1702-3, 1707, 1716, for Kingston 1711, St. Andrew 1720.

Edward Clarke was Member for St. David 1726, died 1731 and buried in the Kingston Parish Churchyard.

Richard Grace was a Churchwarden of St. David 1776.

GUTHRIE vs. SCOTT.

Bill filed 9th June 1720.

Hierome Westhorpe =
of St. Elizabeth, Esq.,
Will dated 1679.

Thomas Nuttall 2nd = Mary = 1st Michael Holsworth
of New York, Gentleman,   of St. Elizabeth, Esq.
married before 1706.

Michael Holsworth and wife left Jamaica for Great Britain but stress of weather compelled them to land at New York where Michael Holsworth died.

Michael Holsworth was Member of the Assembly for St. Elizabeth 1691, 1693, 1695, 1698, for Westmoreland 1703.

GUY vs. JENNINGS.

Bill filed 25th July 1710.

John Hudson Guy = Hannah ——— = 2nd John Jennings
of St. Andrew,   of St. Andrew,
Planter,   gentleman.
d. 9th April 1702.

John Hudson.

John Hudson Guy (Jnr.) is buried in the Cathedral at Spanish Town in the Parish of St. Catherine.

"In this Church lyes interred the body of the Honble. John Hudson Guy, Esqr who departed this life the 7th of Febry. 1749 in the 52nd year of his age, his merit promoted him to several public offices in this Island which he executed with honour and integrity and supported them with dignity; he served his country as a Member of the Assembly, was made an Assistant Judge of the Courts of Law and acted in that station for nine years with so strict an adherence to the rules of justice that he was raised to the Chief Judge's seat as a reward for his uniform and steady regard to the laws of his country."

Arms. Azure, on a chev argent three fleur de lys gules between three Leopards heads or (Lawrence Archer.)

His daughter Elizabeth Hannah (died 5th July 1771) married Chas. Price (afterwards 2nd Baronet) of Jamaica, son of Sir Charles Price (1st Baronet). See Addenda Note 2.

HADEN, JOSEPH (ADMINISTRATOR) VS. CLARKE ET UX ET AL.

Bill filed 20th September 1775.

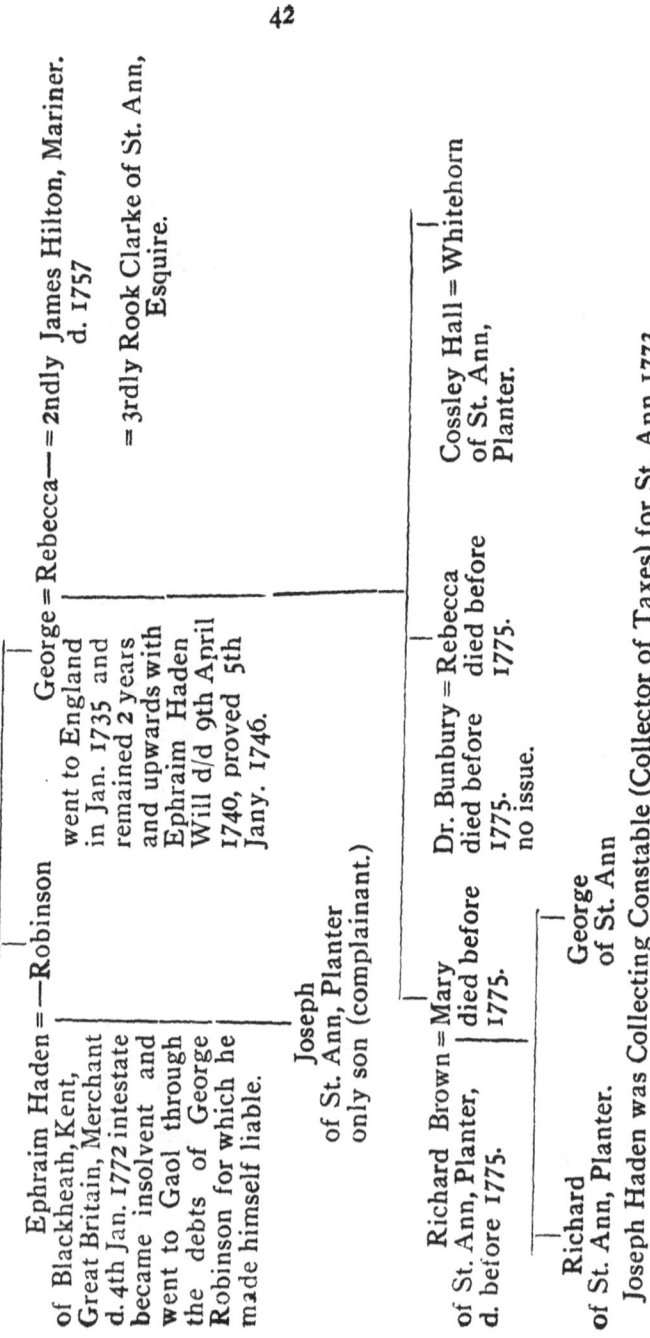

Joseph Haden was Collecting Constable (Collector of Taxes) for St. Ann 1773.

HALHED vs. BARTON.

Bill of Revivor filed July 1766.

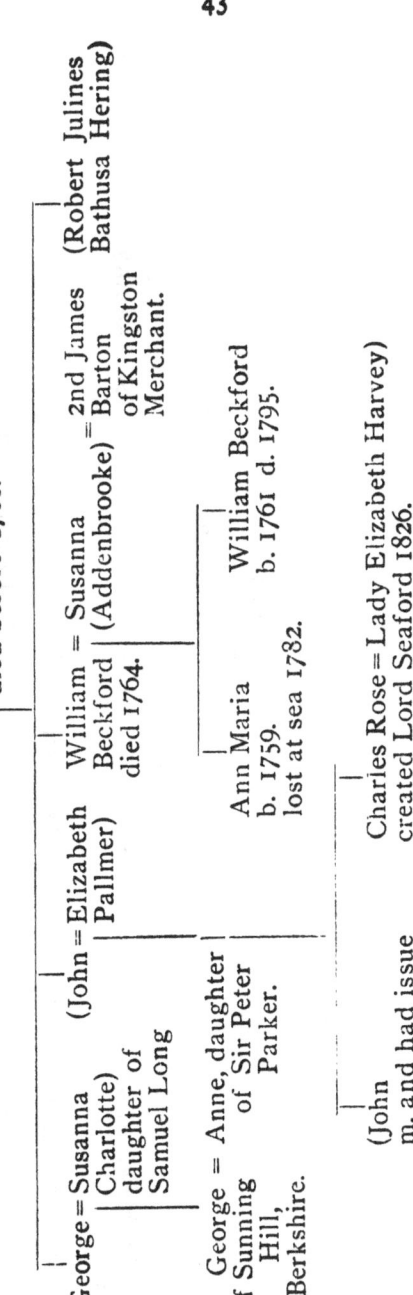

George Ellis, Member of the Assembly, Hanover, 1726-33 appointed Chief Justice of Jamaica 1736, introduced the guinea grass into the Island.

Wm. Beckford Ellis (jnr.) was Member of the Assembly for Portland 1793.

HALSTEAD vs. BROWN.

Bill filed 18th November 1762.

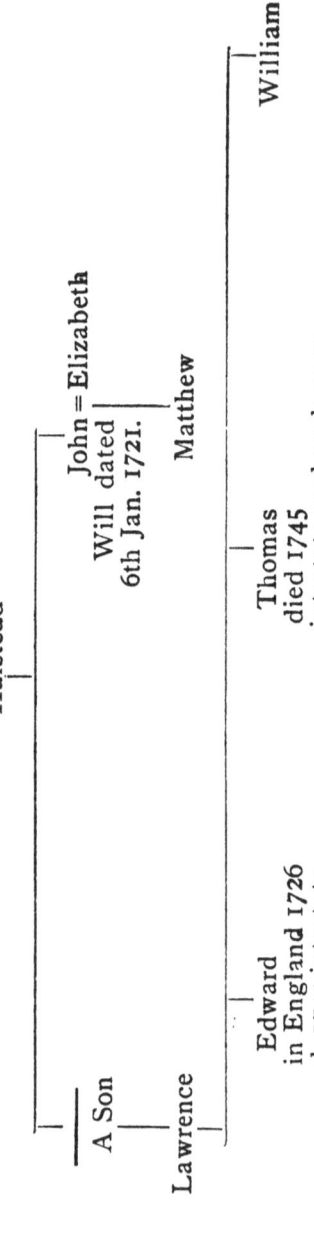

John Halstead was Member of the Assembly for St. John 1706, 1709, St. Dorothy 1719, St. Mary 1721.

Lawrence Halstead was Member of the Assembly for St. Thomas ye Vale 1716.

Matthew Halstead was Member of the Assembly for St. Dorothy 1726.

Edward Halstead is buried in the Cathedral at Spanish Town, St. Catherine's Parish. "Edward Halstead Esqr., Lieut. of ye Troop, son of Lawrence died 25th Dec. 1744 aged 26 (Laurence Archer.)

William Halstead, Member of the Assembly for St. John 1769-1770.

HANSES vs. CAMPBELL.

Bill filed 17th August 1720.

Jacob Allen = Elizabeth = 2ndly in 1714 James Witherington
of St. Elizabeth Planter | d. 1717.   of St. Elizabeth Gentleman.
Will dated Nov. 1713.

Josiah James Hanses = Ann	Elizabeth	Mary Jacob
of St. Thos. in the aged 17		died Augt. 1717
East Esquire. in 1720.		aged 11.

HAUGHTON vs. HAUGHTON (bill filed 17 December 1744).
TAYLOR vs. HAUGHTON (bill filed 20 March 1783).
Jonathan Haughton = 2nd Mary Duhaney.

```
Elizabeth = Richard        Jonathan = 1st Joanna = 2nd Lydia    Philip = (Catherine    Mary = John Ann
m. 2ndly    of Hanover    (b. 17 Dec.   d. 1733    Bowen         died      d. 7 May              Brissett
Edward      Esq., (died   1694, d.      aged 31.   b. 1710       22 Feb.   1775
Clarke of   15 Jan. 1740  18 Feb.                  d. 10 Sept.   1765      aged 60
West-       aged 49).     1767).                   1755.         aged      daughter of
moreland    Owner of                                              64.      Joseph Tharpe)
Esq.        Anglesea Pen
```

(Mary) (Ann)   (Philip, Philip,
                  Jonathan, Sarah,
                  Sarah, Catherine
                  all died young.)

Jonathan Mary Sarah Frances Elizabeth Rebecca = John Waller   (Rachael)   (Elizabeth   (Lydia
d. 24 June m. Dr. m. 1st   nephew of   b. 22 Dec. married   d. young)
1753 aged Wood Col.   John Terrick 1739 died   John
26.   Edward   Bp. of London 23 Feb. 1778 Patterson.)
                 Chambers
                 2nd Litchfield

(Robert = Sarah Garbrand Barrett) (Richard) Elizabeth Goodin = Sir John Taylor
b. 29   d. young   of Parish of St. George
Aug. 1733   Hanover Sq., London.
d. 25 June 1766

Richard Jonathan Philip George Samuel William Elizabeth Helen
d. under d. under   d. under
age.   age.   age.   Elizabeth
```
```

COUNTESS OF HOME vs. EARL OF HOME.
Bill filed 19th August 1752.

COUNTESS DOWAGER OF HUME (HOME?) vs. LUTTRELL.
Bill filed 13th July 1765.

LUTTRELL HON. LADY ELIZABETH vs. EARL OF CARHAMPTON.
Bill filed 20th October 1789.

```
William Gibbons            Sir Nicholas Laws
                           died in Jamaica
                           17 June 1731.
                     ┌─────────────┼─────────────┐
            ┌────────┴────────┐  Temple    Judith Maria = Simon Luttrell
                              │  died                    created Lord
                              │  June 1754               Irnham and
                              │                          afterwards
                              │                          Earl of Car-
                              │                          hampton.
                              │                              │
        ┌─────────────────────┴──┐
2nd = Elizabeth    = 1st James
left Jamaica       of Jamaica Esq.
20 April 1735      married about
20 years of age    1720 died 28 Dec.
when married.      1733, no issue.

William, Earl of Home
married 25 Dec. 1742
deserted his wife
24th Feb. 1743, died
at Gibraltar 28 April
1761.
                                          ┌──────┴───────┬───────┬─────────┬─────────┬──────┐
Henry Lawes  Temple Simon  John  James  Catherine Maria  Elizabeth  Lucy
             came to Jamaica
             1763.

Sir Nicholas Laws was Governor of Jamaica 1718-1722.
```

HUGHES vs. POWELL.

Bill filed 16th July 1752.

(Walter) Hughes
(of Swanzey, Gentleman)

```
[Elizabeth] = Walter         Charles    Stephen      Thomas Powell  2ndly = Alisha ─┬─ 1st Matthew
              of Swanzey                d. before    of St. Andrew                  │   of Kingston
              Wales                     1752.        gentleman                      │   Shipwright,
                                                     a cousin of                    │   (died 1st July
                                                     Matthew Hughes.                │   1744 aged 44).
          │                                                                         │
   ┌──────┴──────┐                      [May = Gamaliel Hughes    Elizabeth]        │
   │             │                                                              (Matthew
 Walter                                                                          b. 16 Oct. 1734
 of Lincolns Inn                                                                 d. 19 Oct. 1737.)
 Co. Middlesex
```

The information in brackets thus [ ] was obtained from the exemplification of the Probate of the Will of Walter Hughes registered in Jamaica 22nd July 1748.

Matthew Hughes was buried in the yard of the Kingston Parish Church.

"Here lie interred the bodies of Matthew Hughes late of this town shipwright (son of Walter Hughes late of ye town of Swanzey in ye Kingdom of Great Britain, gentleman, deceased) who departed this life the 1st of July 1744 aged 44 years and of Matthew his son who was born the 16th of October 1734 and also departed this life the 19th of October 1737."

Arms. A Cheveron between three spears heads. Crest over an Esquire's helmet a deer (?) at gaze. (Lawrence Archer's Monumental Inscription).

JESSOP vs. JOHNSON.

Bill filed 27th September 1764.

―――― Johnson

|
Peter, = Catherine   Elizabeth = John Jessop   Margaret = James Chard   Marian = ―Swanton
of Kingston   of City of Cork   of Cork,   died
Mariner, d.   Ireland, Sailmaker   Ireland,   before
12th May 1751.   m. 13 Nov. 1760.   Shipwright.   1764.

KING vs. PASCO.

Filed 25th January 1766.

```
——— = Thomas King,          ——— = Simon Pasco
      Cooper,                      senior of St. Andrew, Esq.,
      died before 1749.            Will d/d 23 June 1749.
                                   died July 1750.

      Thomas, of Kingston          George
      Gentleman 21 years           of St. Andrew, Esq.
      on 13 Nov. 1765
      nephew of Simon Pasco.
```

LAMOND vs. JACKSON.

Bill filed 16th April 1772.

```
                            Tinling
                               |
         ┌─────────────┬───────┴──────┬──────────────┐
      Patrick    Wm. Bryden    2nd=Alice=1st—Tate    
      of Northum-  of Northum-                        
      berland, Great land Baker                       
      Britain Yeoman. married after                   
                    1769.                             
                                   ┌──────────────┬──────────────┐
                                  Adam         Elizabeth = Andrew Morton
                                  of Kingston                of Northumberland.
                                  Jamaica
                                  Merchant
                                  died 1769.
```

51

LAWRENCE vs. WITTER.

Bill filed 27th July 1764.

Roland Williams of St. James, Esq.
```
         |─────────────────|
    = Joseph              Lewis
      Will dated 1728.
      |────────|
    Lewis    Joseph
    died without issue
    shortly after his father.
```

Roland Williams was Member of the Assembly for Westmoreland 1711, 1718, 1719. St. John 1716 St. Elizabeth 1721, 1722.

Lewis Williams Member of the Assembly Westmoreland 1735.

LITTELJOHN vs. CARGILL.

Bill filed 16th May 1772.

Alexander Graham
of Kingston, Esq.
Will dated 4th Jan. 1760.
|
David Littlejohn = Ann Catherine
of St. Andrew Esq.
|
Amy Elizabeth
died before her Father.

MALCOLM vs. MACKENZIE.

Bill filed 16th August 1766.

```
                John Brissett = Mary ──────── = 2ndly Philip Haughton
                of Hanover Planter                    the younger of
                Will dated 1740.                      Hanover Esq.
          ┌───────────────┤                    ┌──────────────┬──────────────┐
Dr. John Mac-  2nd = Mary = John             George        Haughton      Mary = Neil Malcolm
Kenzie of Hanover.         d. 1760           Richard      died intestate       of Hanover Esq.,
                           intestate.                     and without issue.
                             │
                           John
```

Richard Brissett was Member of the Assembly for Trelawny 1771.

See also suit of Haughton vs. Haughton.

MANN vs. D'WARRIS.

Bill filed 23rd April 1772.

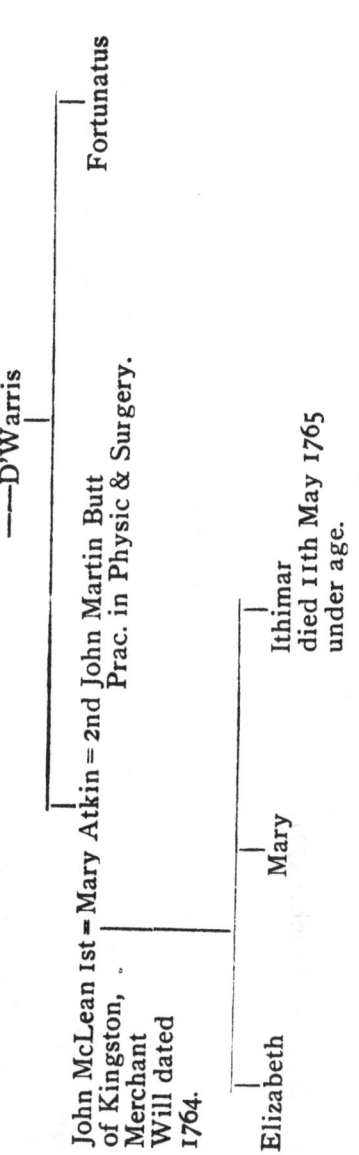

```
                              ———D'Warris
                              |
                                                        |
John McLean 1st = Mary Atkin = 2nd John Martin Butt    Fortunatus
of Kingston,    |             Prac. in Physic & Surgery.
Merchant        |
Will dated      |
1764.           |
        |              |
   Elizabeth         Mary         Ithimar
                                  died 11th May 1765
                                  under age.
```

Fortunatus D'Warris was Member of the Assembly for St. George 1754-5 and afterwards Custos of that Parish. He died 5th February 1790 aged 63. There was a mural tablet to his memory in the Kingston Parish Church.

MEE vs. BLAIR.

Bill filed 30th October 1721.

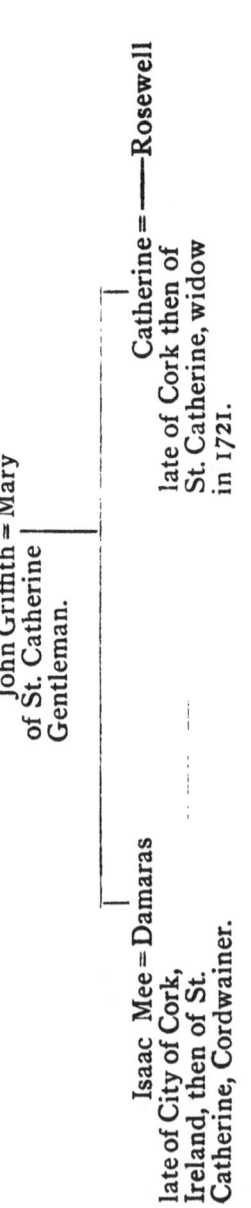

John Griffith = Mary of St. Catherine Gentleman.

Isaac Mee = Damaras late of City of Cork, Ireland, then of St. Catherine, Cordwainer.

Catherine = ——Rosewell late of Cork then of St. Catherine, widow in 1721.

MILLWARD vs. BAYLEY.

Bill filed 1st March 1768.

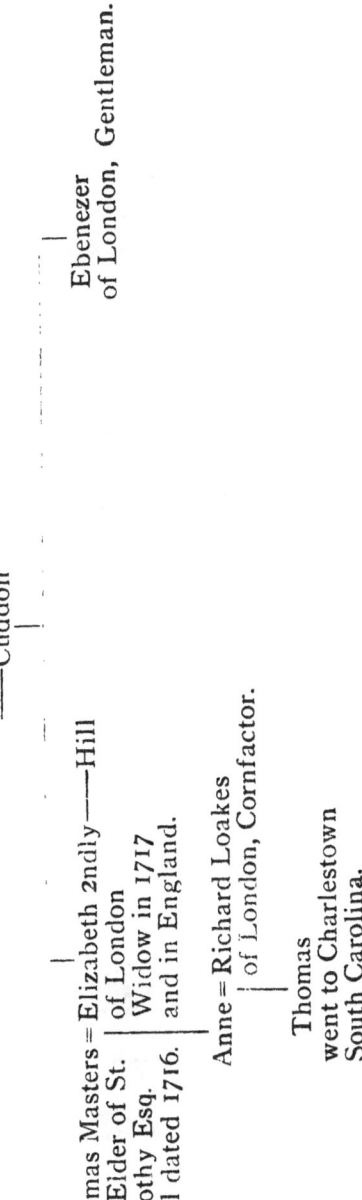

Thomas Masters was in 1710 Member of the Assembly for St. Dorothy.

MOGRIDGE vs. LAWS.

Decree filed 10th July 1721.

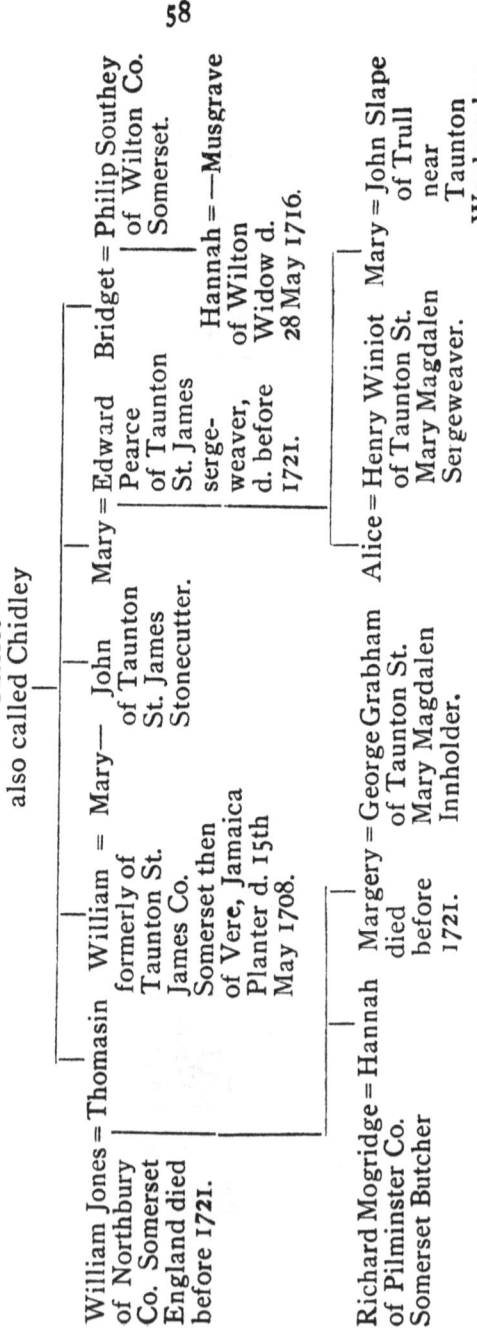

MOORE vs. FENTON.

Bill filed October 24th 1719.

```
John Lenderson = Elizabeth
of St. Andrews   died Dec. 1718.
Planter died 10th
January 1718.
         │
    Anne = Peter Moore
15 in 1719.  of Kingston, Planter
             married 30th June 1719.
```

MOORE vs.

Bill filed 1764.

= John Moore of Westmoreland Esq. in 1731 owned 1200 acres of land in St. James called Montego Bay Will d/d 30 Jan. 1734, died March 1735.

├── John d. 1742 intestate and without issue.

├── Garret d. 1742 intestate and without issue.

├── Francis d. Feb. 1764 intestate and without issue.

Sophia = William of Westmoreland Planter, d. 1738.

William, of Westmoreland Gentleman, only son aged 6 in 1738.

MURE vs. SENIOR.

Bill filed 26th March 1765.

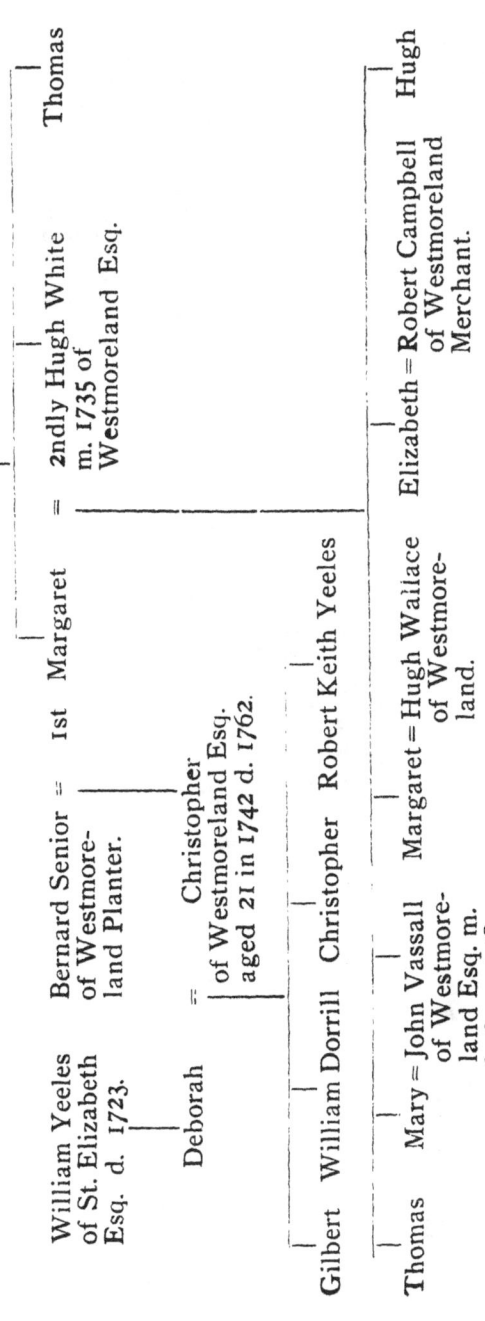

Senior Christopher was Member of the Assembly for Westmoreland 1757.

Wallace Hugh was Member of the Assembly for St. Elizabeth 1767.

White Hugh was Member of the Assembly for Westmoreland 1770.

NICHOLLS vs. WAIGHT.

Bill filed 6th Jan. 1710.

```
                    John Waight = Mary
                    of Port Royal
                    Cordwainer
                    d. 7 June 1692.
         ┌──────────────┬──────────────────┐
   Margaret = —Croft   Frances = Harry Nicholls   Katherine = Richard Mingham
   d. before                    of St. Catherine  d. before   d. before 1697.
   1692.                        gentleman.        1697.
         │                                            │
       Mary                                        Rachael
       d. before                                   d. Feb. 1697
       1692.                                       aged 8 mos.

   ┌─────┐
   John
   d. before
   1692.
```

OSBORN vs. FREEMAN.

Bill filed 20th November 1678.

```
Capt. John Noy 1st = Mary  = 2nd Humphrey Freeman
                     Will dated
                     29 July
                     1678.
        ┌────────────┴────────────┐
    Elizabeth    Grace    (daughter name unknown) = George Osborn
                                                    of Vere, gentleman.
```

PERRY vs. BERNARD.

Bill filed 31 March 1775.

```
                                    Perry
        ┌─────────────────────────────┴──────────────────────────────┐
       Henry                         Jane = Israel Clarke
                                Will dated │ of St. James, Jamaica Esq.
                                     1774. │ Will dated 1765.
         ┌──────────────┬────────────────┬─────────────────┬──────────────┐
     Samuel         Dorothy = John Gill  Sarah    Mary = Samuel Perry   Elizabeth    Jacob Perry
                    formerly of                          of St. Michaels 12 years    10 in 1775.
                    St. Michaels                         Barbadoes,      old in 1775.
                    Barbadoes,                           gentleman.
                    Merchant then
                    of St. Catherine
                    Jamaica gentleman.
```

Jane Clarke and family went to Barbadoes after death of her husband Israel Clarke.

PERSE vs. BATCHELOR.   DARWENT vs. HIGGINS.

Decree filed 18th April 1722.   Bill filed 15th October 1707.

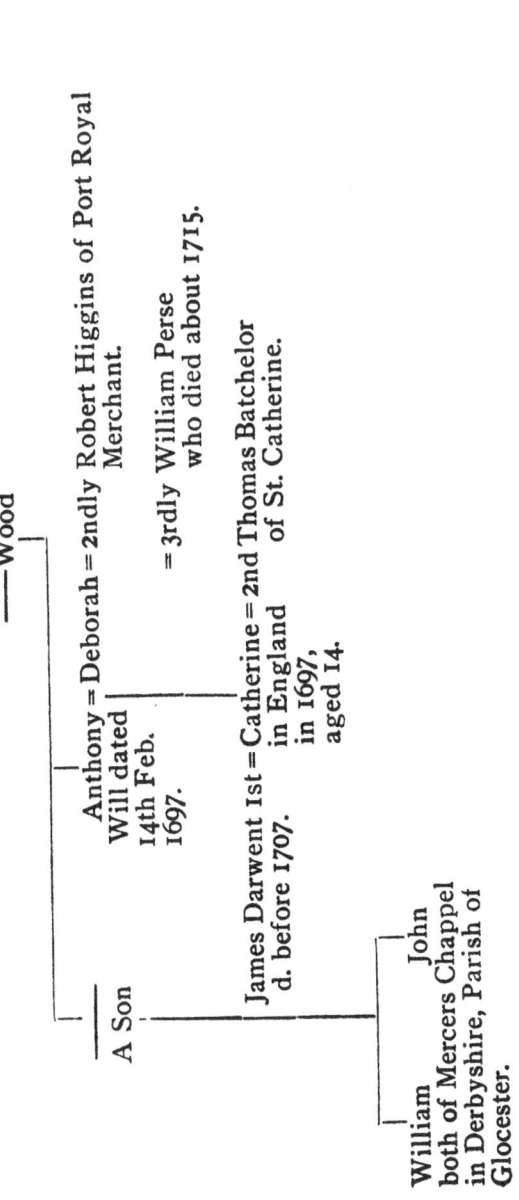

PHILP vs. PUSEY.

Bill filed 18 January 1710.

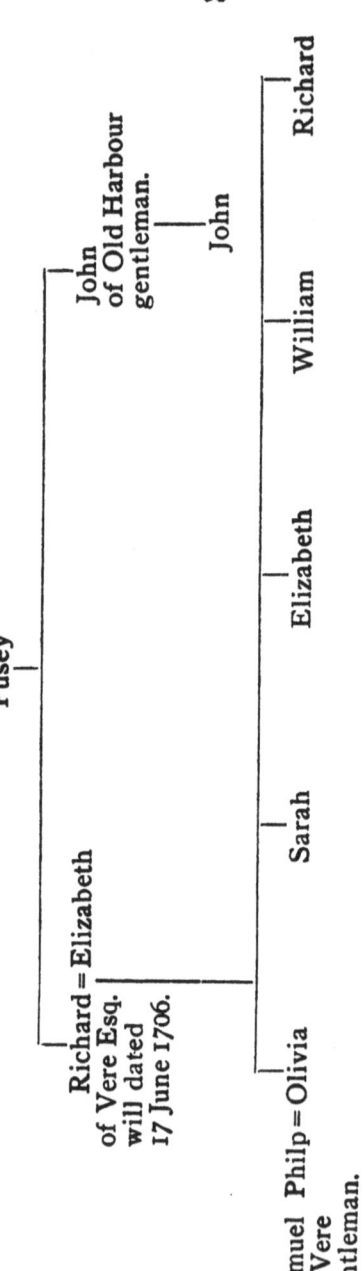

Pusey Richard—Member of the Assembly St. James 1695-1698. Vere 1704.

Pusey John—In the Parish Church of St. Dorothy is memorial to John Pusey Esq. who died 24th January 1767 aged 75 years.
Arms Gules, two bars, or
Crest A Cat o' mountain (Lawrence Archer).

PHIPPS vs. WILLIAMS ET AL.

Bill of Revivor filed 15th November 1764.

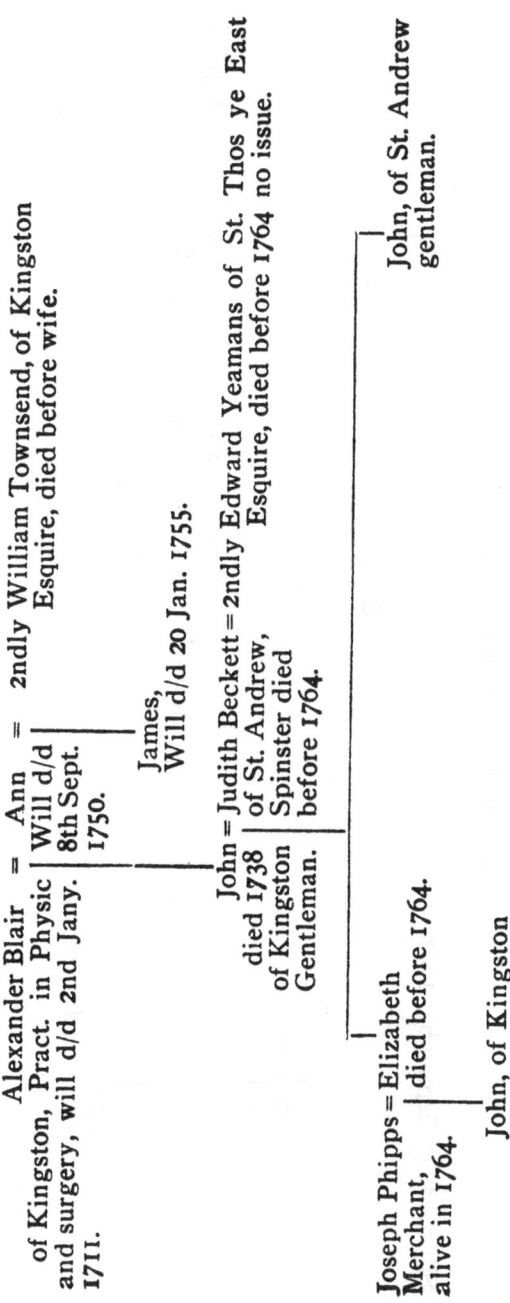

RICHARDSON vs. BECKFORD.

Bill filed 8th September 1742.

```
                    ┌─ Richardson ─┐
                    │              │
         ┌──────────┴──┐      ┌────┴────┐
      Nicholas      Abraham   Richard  Thomas = Ann Elletson = 3rd Edmund Edlyne
                  of St. Catherine Esq.         Will dated 1693 │ widow of Roger E.
                                                                │ of St. Andrew, Esq.
                                                              Mary
```

Richardson Nicholas Member of the Assembly St. Thomas 1691, 1693, 1702, St. David 1695.
    ,,   Thomas Member of the Assembly St. David 1695.

RIDDOCK ET UX VS. FLEMING.

Bill filed 5th December 1765.

William Fleming, of St. Ann Esq. = Elizabeth ──── =2ndly Collin Riddock of St. Ann Pract. in Physic and surgery, in Feb. 1761.
owner of Rio Bueno died Feb. 1760, intestate.

|
William Tinley

Elizabeth = William Tate of St. Ann Merchant.

RIPPON vs. WHINCOP.

Bill filed 22nd April 1719.

Thomas Ashburne
of Kingston Gentleman
Will dated 1712.

```
    |          |         |        |                    |
Thomas   Robert   William    Henry    Mary = Ralph Rippon    Elizabeth
in Great Britain                              of Vere, Planter.
in 1712.
```

Rippon Ralph was Member of the Assembly for Vere 1726–1728 1733 for St. Elizabeth 1731.

ROBERTSON vs. FORBES.

Bill filed 30th August 1770.

```
                    John Robertson = Elizabeth
                    d. 1765          d. March 1759.
      ┌──────────────────┬──────────────────┬──────────────────┬──────────────────┐
  Alexander         Margaret = Robert Mackie    Helen           John            James
  of Kingston,      widow in   of Forres, Co.   of Forres       of London       of Kingston
  gentleman.        1770.      Murray, Scotland                 Merchant        Merchant,
                               Merchant.                        d. Novr. 1759.  arrived 1747
                                                                                d. Jan. 1760.
```

71

RUSSELL vs. BONNOR

Bill filed 11th May 1722.

Doctor John Bonnor died 1708.

```
                    |
         ┌──────────┴──────────┐
       Henry*=                 Margaret = 1st 1684 Joseph Hill, Secretary
         |                              to Governor of Jamaica d. 10 months after
    ┌────┴────┐                         marriage.
 William=Jane  John            2nd John Ashley, of Jamaica Merchant,
 arrived in England                 lived at Port Royal went to England,
 Sept. 1714, died                   wife followed in 1697 and found that
 Dec. 1714 Buried at                a "paraletick appoplectick fitt" had
 St. Mary Ax, Lon-                  deprived him of his senses that he
 don as burial fees                 had been found lunatick and his
 charged.                           brother Walter of Stafford, Clerk, was
                                    Guardian Returned to Jamaica with
                                    wife 1711 Died in Jamaica 1712.

                               3rd William Russell formerly of Jamaica
                                    then of London Gentleman arrived
                                    with wife in England 1713.
```

Bonnor Dr. John—Member of the Assembly for St. Dorothy 1679, 1686, 1693, 1695, 1701, 1703, 1704.
 ,, William—Member of the Assembly for St. Dorothy 1711.

* (See Armstrong vs. Gordon.)

STEWART vs. BRODBELT.

Bill filed 17th April 1770.

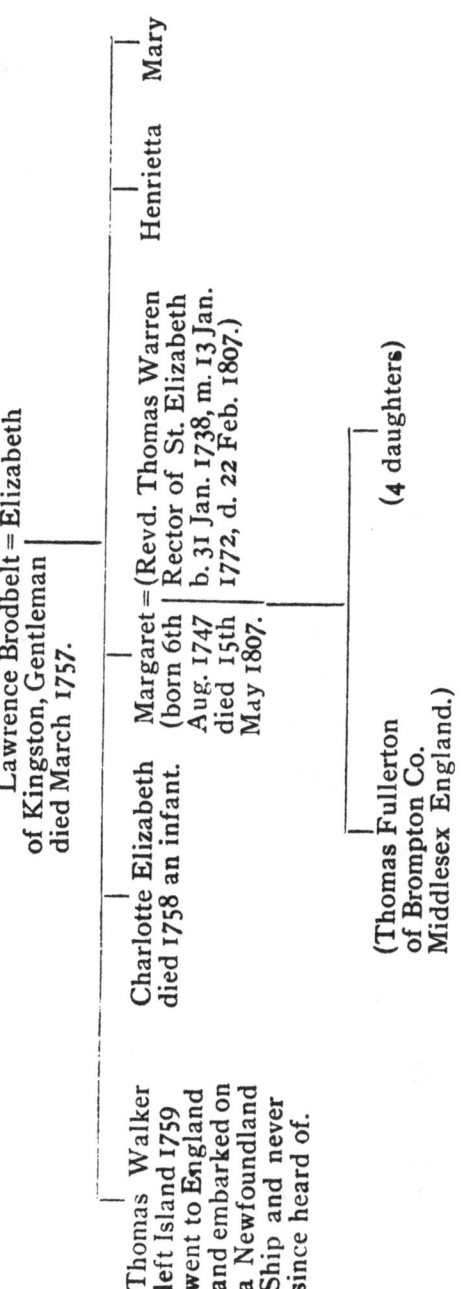

Lawrence Brodbelt = Elizabeth
of Kingston, Gentleman
died March 1757.

| Charlotte Elizabeth died 1758 an infant. | Margaret (born 6th Aug. 1747 died 15th May 1807. | = (Revd. Thomas Warren Rector of St. Elizabeth b. 31 Jan. 1738, m. 13 Jan. 1772, d. 22 Feb. 1807.) | Henrietta | Mary |

Thomas Walker left Island 1759 went to England and embarked on a Newfoundland Ship and never since heard of.

(Thomas Fullerton of Brompton Co. Middlesex England.)   (4 daughters)

There was another family of the same name also settled in Jamaica descended from Daniel Brodbelt, supposed to have been an attaché of the English Embassy in France, who settled here prior to 1739.

SUTTON vs. MOORE.

Bill filed 29th July 1710.

```
         Thomas Sutton = Judith
         of Clarendon Esq.
         died before 1710.
         ┌─────────────┐
       = John         Millethwaite.
        │
       (John)
```

Thomas Sutton was Member of the Assembly for Clarendon 1677-1679, 1686, 1691, 1698, 1701, Vere 1695, Speaker 1691-1693, 1698, Member for Port Royal 1703, 1706. Buried in Parish Church at Vere "Here lyeth inter'd the body of Coll Thomas Sutton who departed this life the 15th day of November in the seventy second year of his age and in the year of our Lord God 1710.

John Sutton, grandson of above is also interred in same Church. He died 23rd August 1745.

TAYLOR vs. GREGORY.

Answer filed 2nd November 1764.

ELLETSON vs. TAYLOR.

Bill filed 20th June 1769.

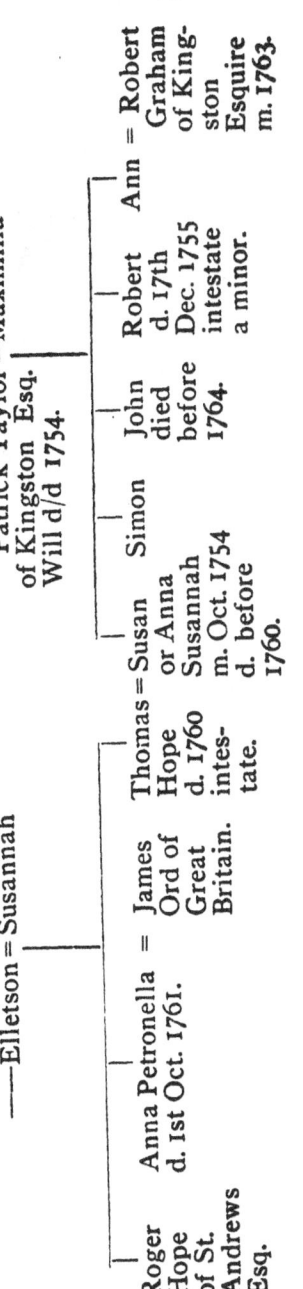

Elletson.—Roger Hope Elletson was Lieutenant Governor of Jamaica in 1766 and resided at Hope Estate in St. Andrews—the Elletson Road in Kingston was originally a private road leading from the Hope Estate to the shore of Kingston Harbour down which the produce of the Estate was brought and shipped from a wharf at the end of the road.

Thomas Hope Elletson was Member of the Assembly for St. Andrew 1754-55 and St. George 1756.

Ord James was Member of the Assembly for Kingston 1744-45, 1749-50.

Taylor Patrick—Member of the Assembly for St. George 1753.

VASSALL vs. STOUT.

Filed ———

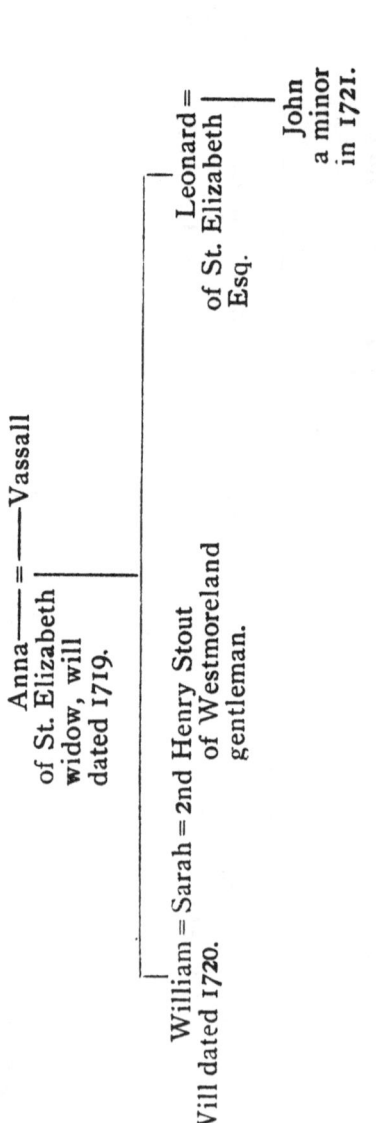

```
        Anna ———— = ———— Vassall
     of St. Elizabeth
     widow, will
     dated 1719.
     ┌─────────────────────────┬──────────────────┐
William = Sarah = 2nd Henry Stout         Leonard =
Will dated 1720.   of Westmoreland     of St. Elizabeth
St. Ann 1709, '13, St. David 1718, 1719.  Esq.
                   gentleman.              │
                                          John
                                       a minor
                                        in 1721.
```

William Vassall was Member of the Assembly for St. Elizabeth 1703, St. Mary 1707, Westmoreland 1705, St. Ann 1709, '13, St. David 1718, 1719.

Henry Stout was Member of the Assembly for St. Elizabeth 1722, Westmoreland 1724 and a Member of the Council 1726.

WALLIN vs. BOURKE.

Bill filed 1st August 1770.

John Wallin = Mary = 2ndly James Trowers
of St. Catherine Esq.   of St. Catherine Esq.
d. 7th July 1750.

— John, died before 1750.
— Richard of St. Catherine Esq. educated in England returned 1752.
— Lydia

WIGNALL vs. HALL.

Bill filed 5th January 1774.

```
(Edmund Hall = (Anne, daughter of John Elmers Esq.     (William Wyatt = Elizabeth, daughter of
 of Greatford Hall    of Swinford.)                                      Edward Heylin.)
 Lincolnshire.)
                |                                                |
                William Hall = Elizabeth = 2ndly ——— Humphrey
                owner of Halls Delight,   died Dec. 1722.
                St. Andrew, then a sugar
                work, died 18th Sept.
                1699 (youngest son) (m.
                26 July 1688.)
    |                    |                    |                         |
James = Elizabeth   Frances = Dr. Richard Owen   Rachael = Richard   Anna Maria = Eleazer Wignall
died                both died before 1774.                Basnett     of St. Thos.    Esq.
Novr.                                                     Esq. d.     ye East, 18
1742.                                                     before      years old in
                                                          1774.       1711.
                                                                      |
                                                                Richard    John
```

Eleazer Wignall was Member of the Assembly for St. David 1678–9. St. Thos ye East 1737. Died 1743. William Hall appointed his well beloved friends Lieut. Col. Thomas Clarke, Captain Joseph Sergeant, and his cousin George Brailsford all of Jamaica and Mr. Le Peyser of England Executors.

WILKINS vs. GALE.

Bill filed 15th March 1739.

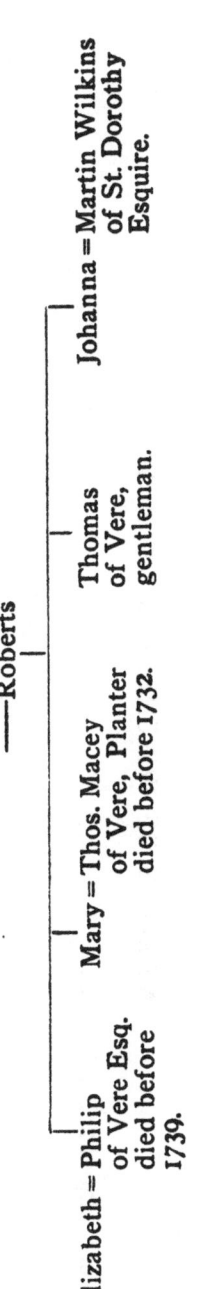

```
                    ———Roberts———
        |              |            |            |
Elizabeth = Philip   Mary = Thos. Macey   Thomas    Johanna = Martin Wilkins
of Vere Esq.         of Vere, Planter     of Vere,           of St. Dorothy
died before          died before 1732.    gentleman.         Esquire.
1739.
```

MARQUIS OF WINCHESTER vs. HEYWOOD

Decree dated 2nd July 1722.

John, Lord Vaughan
Earl of Carbery.
_____
Anne = Rt. Hon. Charles Lord Pawlett
Marquis of Winchester.

Lord Vaughan was Governor of Jamaica 1675–1678.

PART II.

A PROCLAMATION FOR THE ENCOURAGING OF PLANTERS IN HIS MAJESTY'S ISLAND OF JAMAICA IN THE WEST INDIES.

1661.

WEE being fully satisfied that Our 'Island of Jamaica, being a pleasant and most fertile soyle, and scituate commodiously for trade and commerce, is likely, through God's blessing, to be a greate benefitt and advantage to this and other our Kingdoms and dominions, have thought fitt, for encourageing of our subjects, as well such as are already upon the said Island, as all others that shall transport themselves thither, and reside and plant there, to declare and publish, and wee do hereby declare and publish, That thirtie acres of improveable lands shall be granted and allotted to every such person, male or female, being twelve years old or upwards, who now resides, or within two years next ensuing shall reside, upon the said Island; and that the same shall be assigned and sett out by the the Governor and Council within six weeks next after notice shall bee given, in writing, subscribed by such planter or planters or some of them in behalfe of the rest to the Governor or such Officer as he shall appoint in that behalfe, signifying their resolution to plant there, and when they intend to bee on the place: and in case they do not go thither within six months then next ensuing, the said allotment shall be void, and free to bee assigned to any other planter; and that every person or persons to whom such assignment shall bee made, shall hold and enjoy the said lands soe to be assigned, and all houses, edifices, buildings and enclosures thereupon to bee built or made, to them and their heirs for ever by and under such tenures as is usual in other plantations subject to us. Neverthelesse, they are to bee obliged to serve in armes upon any insurrection, mutiny, or forraine invasion; and that the said assignments and allotments shall be made and confirmed under the publique seal of the said Island, with power to create any mannor or mannors, and with such convenient and suitable privileges imunities as the grantee shall reasonably desire and require; and a draught of such assignment shall bee prepared by our learned Councell in the lawe and delivered to the Governor to that purpose; and that all fishings and piscaries, and all copper, lead, tin, iron, coales, and all other mines (except gold and silver) within such respective allotments, shall be enjoyed by the grantees thereof, reserving only a twentieth part of the product of the said mines to our use. AND wee do further publish and declare, That all children of any of our natturall borne subjects of England to bee borne in Jamaica, shall, from their respective births, bee reputed to bee, and shall bee, free denizens of England, and shall have the same privileges, to all intents and purposes as our free borne subjects of Englahd; and that all free persons shall have libertie, without interruption, to transport themselves and their families, and any of their goods (except only coyne and bullion) from any our Dominions and territories to the said Island of Jamaica AND wee do strictly charge and command all planters, soldiers. and others, upon the said Island, to yield obedience to the lawfull commands of our right trusty and well beloved Thomas Lord Windsor, now our Governor of our said Island, and to every other Governor thereof for the tyme being, under paine of our displeasure, and such penalties as may be inflicted thereupon.

>Given at our Courte at Whitehall the fourteenth day of December

>>p.ipm. regem.

PART III.

A SHORT ACCOUNT OF JAMAICA WHEN SIR CHARLES LITTLETON LEFT IT IN THE YEAR 1664 WHICH BY HIS MAJESTY'S COMMAND HE PRESENTED TO THE PRIVY COUNCIL.

A SHORT ACCOUNT OF JAMAICA WHEN SIR CHARLES LITTLETON LEFT IT IN THE YEAR 1664 WHICH BY HIS MAJESTY'S COMMAND HE PRESENTED TO THE PRIVY COUNCIL.

He left the Government in the Council, who chose Colonel Lynch President, to whom he also gave a commission to command all the forces, and to be a Judge of the Courts of Justice with some Assistants.

THE SITUATION.

It lies in the Northern Latitude of 17 and 18 degrees, in the Heart of all the Spanish Dominions and therefore fittest to be made the seate for commerce and Trade and if a War be intended it is the most advantageously seated of all the Islands in these parts for between the East end of Jamaica and the West of Hispaniola which is about 20 leagues distance, is the passage for all the Spaniards that Trade from St. Domingo, Porto Rico, and the Carraccas &c., to the Havana and all Cuba and Nova Hispania, and between the West of Cuba, which is the Cape Antoine, and the Cape Cattoche upon the Main (where begins the Bay of Mexico and is but 50 leagues from Cape to Cape) is the Passage for all the Galleons with the Plate Fleet, from Peru to come to the Havana, where is the Rendez vous for all the King of Spains Fleet before they pass the Gulf of Florida to return into Europe, and between these Capes our men of war do constantly ply, and can easily get up to Jamaica. Jamaica is about 80 Leagues from the Main, and beareth from Rio de Hatah N. W. 150 Leagues, From St. Marth N. N. W. 135 Leagues Rio Grand N. W. 130 Leagues Carthagena N. 144 L. Porto Bello N. E. 6 N. 180 Leagues. From Gratias a Dios E b. N. 80 L. The Bay of Mexico E. 130 L.

THE CONVENIENCY OF HARBOUR.

To the East lies Port Morant, 14 Leagues to Leeward is thePoint Cagua, or Port Royal, worthily so named for the Goodness and Largeness of the Harbour, where all the Kings Fleet may ride, and the best of them close aboard the shore to lade or unlade, the most securely. Here all the Merchants lived as being the only place of Trade. At this Port is the only Fort of Strength in the Island and was when Sir Charles Littleton left it, not above one third finished, which if faithfully laid out may be so for £2000 its built of very good stone and irregular, when tis finished will be of sufficient strength to secure the Harbour and to defend itself, because it can be difficultly approached, Garrison Soldiers being supposed to maintain it, for the Inhabitants are not to be relied on, nor were enough to defend it, there will be about 40 pieces of Ordnance upon it, and most of them very good guns, as well Brass as Iron, this Port cannot be asssisted by the Island settlements they are at so great a distance and the way easily cut off from them, about 5 Leagues Leeward is another Harbour called the Old Harbour which is not easy to come into, nor so safe riding—further Leeward is Maccary Bay where small vessels do commonly ride and Blewfields Bay where all Ships that are Homewards bound do commonly wood and water, and is a very good Harbour—on the North side of the Island is Port Antonio, and Rio Novo where the Spaniards last landed with 800 men, and fortified, but were bravely beaten out by Coll Doyley then Governor. There is also on this side Montegua Bay and other good Harbours.

THE STRENGTH AND NUMBER OF THE INHABITANTS AND THEIR SETTLEMENTS.

The Regiment of Port Morant and Yellows* was commanded by Colonel Lynch, and was at that time the best and richest Province.

Over the Regiment of Ligonea, which was the fastest and strongest quarter in the Island, and also the most numerous Colonel Barry was Colonel.

Over the Four Companies at Port Royal, Capt Jno Man did command there being no Field Officer left.

The Regiment at the Old Spanish Town (called St. Jago) and the Angels Old Harbour Passage Fort and Places adjacent which was Sir Charles Littleton's Regiment Major Fuller commanded.

At Guanna Boa and the large Precincts thereof is the Regiment commanded by Lt Colonel Cope and Major Ivy.

There Regiments by their several lists, and the strictest accounts could be made were judged to make in all 2500 men and the Hunters and other unsettled people not listed in any Musters dispersed over the several Quarters some 4 or 500 more, besides women and children, of these there may be found upon occasion some 150 on Horseback well enough furnished, with saddles arms &c.

The Foot were very ill armed, especially with Muskets, and Pikes, are of small use in that Place where they are not like to deal with Horse, and the ways narrow, and full of High Wood. What force there is, is to be dispersed, they can but difficultly rendezvous to join in a Body.

---
* Yallahs.

The Interest of this Island as of all New Settlements is daily changing—Provisions and all sorts of goods of the Country Produce being infinitely increased in that two years space which Sir Charles Littleton stayed there, before which time they little intended Planting or Breeding of Cattle.

The Designs of a Free Trade can hardly be effectual but by order from Spain nor the Privateers called in, but (and that difficultly) by Frigates from England, the English being grown so hateful to the Spaniards in those parts, they would scarce receive the very Friars and other Prisoners were sent home to them. We had then in their coasts about 14 or 15 Sail of Privateers, in them 1500 or 2000 Seamen, few of which take Order but from stronger Men of War and as it hath been always their trade and livelihood, and they being of several Nations, if we forbid them our Ports they will go to others, to the French and Dutch, and find themselves welcome enough.

The Government of the Island was plain and agreeable, so were the Laws and Execution neither Merchants or Planters seemed dissatisfied every Cause or Law suit being determined in 6 weeks with 30 or 40 charges.

The People were generally easy to be governed yet rather by Persuasion than severity. The attemps by Captain Minors upon the Spaniards and Privateering had lett out the many ill Humours, and those that remained were in ways of thriving, and by that mode peaceable and industrious.

PART IV.

PROPOSITIONS FOR THE SPEEDY SETTLING OF JAMAICA.

PROPOSITIONS FOR THE SPEEDY SETTLING OF JAMAICA.

Imprimis.

That His Majesty be pleased by His Royal Proclamation to declare this Island to belong to the Crown of England, and that he holds himself obliged to protect his good subjects there, in their Possessions and Estates, and in their Laws and just Liberties as fully and amply as the subjects of any other His Majesty's Realms and Dominions and that he nor his Successors will impose any Tax Talliage Cost Subsidy Loan or any other charge upon them without the consent of the Major Part of the Representatives of the Freeholders of that his Island according to their usual manner (by his Royal Writs) assembled.

ITEM.

That it may be lawful for His Majesty's Authority here to admit any Persons of what Nation soever with their Families to settle and plant in this Island, and that for their Encouragement the Governor and Council may have full power to naturalize them for this Island only, whereby they may enjoy only within the same Laws Liberties and Privileges of natural born Englishmen.

ITEM.

That His Majesty be pleased to continue the allowance of Liberty of Conscience, and a free exercise of Religion to all Persons settled there, according to their several Persuasion in the same manner as by His Majestys Grace, now they enjoy the same.

These three being granted, and sufficiently manifested to the World will be Encouragement enough to gain Inhabitants hither for the Goodness of the Soil is now so well known that there will need no other Invitation but the above Assurance of Protection and Freedom &c.

ITEM.

That all prudential means be used to encourage the Scots to come hither and being very good servants, and to prevent them from going to Poland and other Nations whereby they are absolutely lost to His Majestys service which as in that, so in all other His Majesty's Dominions is of greatest importance, for.........................could the Increase of His Majestys native subjects be made Artificiers at Home or sent to His Majesty's Foreign Plantations abroad, all sorts of Commodities and Merchandize would be so plentiful and cheap as that the unusual Trade would be scarcely restored to our Nation without a blow.

ITEM.

For the Further Increase of His Majesty's subjects We may have License gratis, or at some moderate Rates to trade for Negroes in Affrick, giving security to carry them to no other Market but this.

Did those Honourable Persons which make that Royal Company so glorious, but fall into consideration how much more it is His Majesty's Interest to increase the numbers of his subects, than Bullion of Gold or Silver (which by law all Nations may import) they would not only freely consent to this Proposal for us, but for the whole Nation and Foreigners also—

Mankind is the principal, Gold the Accessory increase the...........................and the other must follow—I (for my twenty-four years experience in the Indies) affirming that Barbados had never rise to that Perfection we have lately seen it in, had it not been lawful for Dutch, Hamburghers our own whole Nation and any other to bring and sell them Blacks or any other Servants in their Infancy.

ITEM.

That we may have a Coin allowed us either by a Mint set up here with His Majestys Directions for its weight and Alloy or the like in England for coining such gold and silver as shall be....................by Order of the Persons interested in this Place, with a particular mark on it and Power to export it, or if neither of these may be permitted that our Agent may have License to export to this Island, so much of the now English coin, as we import Bullion otherwise we shall have no true measure of Things, and be very much impeded and embroiled in our Trade which the jealous Spaniard allows in the Indies, as essentially necessary to their traffic, though in most other things he be austerely reserved in his no small Prejudice.

Lastly—That the Laws made by the Assembly here long since sent home to the late Lord Chancellor, to be presented to His Majesty for His Royal Assent, may be returned hither confirmed by His Majesty under the Great Seal, or at least so many of them as His Majesty shall approve of.

PART V.
LIST OF THE TRAINED BANDS TAKEN IN JUNE 1670.

A LIST OF THE TRAINED BANDS TAKEN IN JUNE 1670.

Captains, names of each Company	Private Soldiers in each company	Infty. Officers in Company	The Number of Soldiers in each Regiment	The number of Officers in each Regiment	The whole of Soldiers and Officers in the Island of Jamaica.
The General's Compy.	182	18			
Lt. Coll. Jno. Cope	36	6			
Capt. Walrond	83	7			
Capt. Aylemore	30	6	The General's Regiment.		
Capt. Richd. Oldfield	55	7	717	73	790
Capt. Jno. Langley	62	6			
Capt. John Bourden	108	8			
Major Thos. Fuller	115	9			
Capt. Wm. Moseley	46	6			

Captains, names of each Company	Private Soldiers in each Company	Infty. Officers in Company	The Number of Soldiers in each Regiment	The number of Officers in each Regiment	The whole of Soldiers and Officers in the Island of Jamaica.
Col. Freeman's Regiment.					
Col. Thos. Freeman	48	7			
Lt. Col. Robert Freeman	49	6			
Capt. Thomas Browne	45	6			
Capt. Jno. Holley	36	6			
Capt. Nicholas Alexander	37	8	251	40	291
Capt. Atkins	36	7			
The Leeward Regiment.					
Lt. Col. Wm. Ivy	64	8			
Major Anthony Collier	96	8			
Saml. Long Capt.	48	7			
Capt. Horner	80	7	334	38	372
Capt. Parker & Co. of Dragoons	46	8			

To which add the Capts. which are 2354 / 32

Foot Soldiers 2386

Captains, names of each Company	Private Soldiers in each Company	Infty. Officers in Company	Regiment	The Number of Soldiers in each Regiment	The Number of Officers in each Regiment	The whole of Soldiers and Officers in the Island of Jamaica.
Lt. General's Company	54	9	Lt. General's Regiment			
Lt. Coll. Hope	67	9				
Major Whitfield	56	8				
Capt. Vallet	51	6		340	47	387
Capt. Peace	62	7				
Capt. Saml. Warner	50	8				
The Major General's Compy.	102	10	Major General's Regiment			
Lt. Coll. Byndloss	96	10				
Major Wm. Beeston	125	10		464	50	514
Captain Keene	88	10				
Capt. Edgegoose	53	10				

Captains, names of each Company.	Private Soldiers in each Company.	Infty. Officers Soldiers in each	The Officers in each Regiment.	The number Officers in each Regiment	The whole of Soldiers and Officers in the Island of Jamaica.
Lt. Col. Thos. Ballard—Horse	60	6			
Major Thos. Ayscough	36	5	The Horse Regiment 192	24	216
Capt. Samuel Barry	51	9			
Capt. Gifford Pennant	27	5			
Major Loyds old troop	18	2			
Capt. Cooper and Capt. Jenkes two Companies on the Northside 100		10			110
					2712
					8
To which add the Captains of the Horse and the two northside Captains					2720

PART VI.

A LIST OF THE SHIPS UNDER THE COMMAND OF ADMIRAL MORGAN.

A LIST OF THE SHIPS UNDER THE COMMAND OF ADMIRAL MORGAN.

Ships Names.	Commanders.	Tons.	Guns.	Man.
The Satisfaction Frigate	Admiral Henry Morgan	120	22	140
The Mary Frigate	Captain Thomas Harris	50	12	70
The May Flower	Captain Joseph Bradley	70	14	100
The Pearle	Captain Lawrence Prince	50	12	70
Civillian	Capt. Erasmus	80	12	75
Dolphin Frigate	Capt. Jno. Morris	60	10	60
Lilly Frigate	Captain Richard Norman	50	10	50
Port Royal	Capt. James Delliatt	50	12	55
The Gift	Capt. Thomas Rogers	40	12	60
John of Vaughall	Capt. Jno. Pyne	70	6	60
The Thomas	Capt. Hump. Throston	50	8	45
The Fortune	Captain Richard Ludbury	40	6	40
Constant Thomas	Capt. Coone Darlvaunce	60	6	40
The Fortune	Capt. Richd. Dobson	25	6	35
The Prosperous	Capt. Henry Wills	16	4	35
Abraham Offeranda	Capt. Richard Taylor	60	4	30
Virgin Queen	Capt. Jno. Bennet	15	—	30
Recovery	Capt. Jno. Shepherd	18	3	30
The Sloop Wm.	Capt. Thos. Woodriffe	12	—	30
The Billy Sloop	Capt. William Curson	12	—	25
The Fortune	Capt. Clement Symons	40	4	40
The Endeavour	Capt. Geo. Hammanson	25	4	35
Bonadventure	Capt. Roger Taylor	20	—	25
Prosperous	Capt. Patrick Dunbar	10	—	16
Endeavour	Capt. Charles Swan	16	2	30
The Lambe Sloop	Capt. Richd. Powell	30	4	30
Fortune	Capt. Jones Reekes	16	3	30
The Free Gift	Roger Kelly	15	4	40
		1120	180	1326

Ships Names.	Commanders.	Tons.	Guns.	Man.
FRENCH SHIPS.				
St. Catherine	Capt. Tribiter	100	14	110
Galliandena	Capt. Gascoone	80	10	80
St. Jno.	Capt. Diego	80	10	80
St. Peter	Capt. Pearse Hantot	80	10	90
Le Deauble Volant	Capt. Desnaugla	40	6	50
Le Levsa Sloop	Capt. Joseph	25	2	40
Le Lyon Sloop	Capt. Charles	30	3	40
Le St. Maria	Capt. Jno. Linaux	30	4	30
		1585	59	520
	English ships in all	28	180	1326
	French ships in all	8	59	520
		36	239	1846

PART VII.

REPORT BY SIR THOMAS MODYFORD TO THE LORD ARLINGTON, DATED 23RD SEPTEMBER 1670.

SIR THOMAS MODYFORD TO THE LORD ARLINGTON.

JAMAICA
23rd September 1670.

May it please Your Lordship.

By the extraordinary diligence of His Majesty's Receiver General I have recovered the promised Survey the which I could wish were perfect, however this will give Your Lordship some Light of this place, which I hope betwixt this and March to reduce to a more certainty, as is the promise.

Your Lordship will find great quantities of land granted to some persons among whom my Son 6,000 acres whose name I made use of for myself having about 400 Persons in Our Family and so but one half acre due. 5,000 to Capt. Noy which is the Wast Land by the Sea Side, most part covered with Salt Water where is a very hopeful work began for Salt etc.

There is 3,200 to one Styles, who never had hands proportionable, nor ever will as I judge, but the reasons of it was that within a year of my coming he made oath His Majesty had granted a Privy Seal for that Quantity which he had lost by the War and faithfully promised to stock it which being when nobody would take lands I granted it and desire Your Lordship to direct my son to search the Privy Seal Office, whether there be any such grant.

As to the rest the Proportion of Hands is not wanting or for its security and in the whole grant added together Your Lordship will find double the number. I humbly beg Your Lordship's excuses for the Haste and that you would be pleased to own me.

Your most faithful and obedient servt.,

THOS. MODYFORD,

PART VIII.

SURVEY OF THE ISLAND.

NOTE.—Names marked * indicate that same were undecipherable.

III

SURVEY.

ST. THOMAS PARISH.

	acres
Thomas Amor	10
Southwell Alkins Esqr.	1070
Chas. Barnett	90
John Basser	78
Thomas Booth	12
William Basnett	60
Captain Thomas Brenne	1060
Joseph Barger	11
Francis Butterfield	30
Samuel Backs Esq.	250
Christopher Cooper	690
Cæsar Carter	60
Garvell Crouch	100
Thomas Carpenter	6
John Clarke	90
Josiah Child and Mate	1330
Jno. Devenport	340
Francis Davis	120
Thomas Evans	215
Stephen Evans	330
Col. Thos. Freeman	1309½
Robert Fargasson	24
James Gosling	800
*Thomas G.........	238
Jno. Hooper	140
Jno. Hunt	180
Thos. Hudson	390
More	120
David Innes	70
Thomas Johnson	350
Widdow Lawrence	73
Henry Lupton	450
Jno. Lucy	92
Richard Layton	90
Nicholas License	264

		acres.
Samuel Lewis Esq.	... ...	880
Edward Madox	... ...	30
Thos. Manning	... ...	125
Danl. Pearce	... ...	8
Charles Probert	... ...	64
Rice Prossen	... ...	700
Jno. Petgrave	... ...	38
Jno. Putnam	... ...	200
Dearman Regain	... ...	145
More	... ...	40
George Robbins	... .	12
Thomas Reese	... ...	60
Clement Richardson	... ...	10
Jno. Stokes	... ...	25
Jno. Stevenson	... ...	211
Edmund Sweet	... ...	140
Thos. Stacey	... ...	120
James Scott	... ...	17
Thos. Stevens	... ...	60
Jno. Stevens	... ...	60
Jno. Salisbury	... ...	156
Walter Tresias	... ...	120
Tobias Walton	... ...	50
Thomas Wiltshire	... ...	122
Jno. Wallis and Boucher	... ...	150

In this Parish are Families 59
and by estimation People 590

ST. DAVID'S PARISH.

Nicholas Alexander	... ...	760
Robert Avery	... ...	30
Thomas Bend	... ...	80
Edwd. Bates	... ...	49
Jno. Benton	... ...	150
Jno. Bayfield	... ...	60
Jas. Campion	... ...	90
More	... ...	13
Cornelius Cole	... ...	90
Henry Cole	... ...	30

		acres.
William Davis	... ...	156
Thomas Evans and mate	... ...	160
Geo. Elkins & Petty ...	... ...	563
Edwd. Elliot & Pearse	... ...	80
Francis Fowsacers ...	... ...	160
Lt. Coll. Robt. Freeman	... ...	1338¾
Coll. Thos. Freeman ...	... ...	440
Edward Fox	... ...	90
Thomas Fargar	... ...	345
Richard Gomersell	... ...	140
Morgan George	... ...	30
Thos. Griffin	... ...	15
Matthew Halpen	... ...	60
Jno. Harris	... ...	60
Thos. Harry	... ...	120
Geo. Hooke	... ...	90
Henry Henderson	... ...	30
John Hobby and Alexander	... ...	82
Jno. Hobby	... ...	126
Geo. Hunt	... ...	45
Jno. Haldins	... ...	30
Saml. Hancock	... ...	60
Jno. James & Mate	... ...	70
Edwd. Jackson	... ...	30
Peter Jacob	... ...	30
John Gerrard & Jourden	... ...	30
Jno. Lawstead	... ...	30
Major Richard Loyd ...	... ...	1370
Major Loyd & Burton ...	... ...	294
Bryan Mascall & Sylvester	... ...	34
Matthew Oliver	... ...	30
Luke Phillips	... ...	150
Henry Poores	... ...	40
John Price	... ...	140
Francis Powell	... ...	17
Richard Pearce and Elliott	... ...	10
Matt Price	... ...	60

		acres.
Robert Puncher	... ...	60
Willm. Powell	... ...	30
Wm. Ring	... ...	70½
William Rives Esq.	... ...	210
Walter Roles	... ...	40
Richard Richardson Esq.	... ...	1034
Richard Richardson & Mate	... ...	152
Edward Rice	... .	30
Thos. Reel	... ...	150
Jas. Rogers	... ...	30
Clement Richardson	... ...	50
Thomas Ramsdon	... ...	130
Robert Stubs and mate	... ...	66
Jacob Stokes	... ...	640
Jacob Stokes and Smith	... ...	1
Willm. Sheldrake	... ...	35
Benjm. Smith	... ...	60
Robt. Smith	... ...	374
Major Jno. Sanderson	... ...	44
*Thomas S..........	... ...	60
John Terry	... ...	58
Jenkin Thomas	... ...	18½
Charles Thomas	... ...	30
Robt. Thompson	... ...	35
Stephen Valley	... ...	35
Thomas Whittle	... ...	60
William Wolfe	... ...	30
Henry Winkey and mate	... ...	65
Jas. Wallis	... ...	30
Robt. Woddard	... ...	60
William Witch	... ...	30
John Wilson and Willm. Parker	... ...	30
John White and Elkin ...	... ...	30
John Wimble and Seamore	... ...	152

    In this Parish are Families   80
    and by estimation persons   960

ST. ANDREW'S PARISH.

	acres.
Jno. Andrews	4
Heny Archbould Esqr.	2030
Thos. Aldworth	5
Jno. Akin	7½
Jas. Bonnet	5
Edwd. Bussell	11
Robt. Bull	34
Charles Bermay	30
Doctr. Richd. Brian	351
Jas. Barrett and mates	90
Nicholas Barrett and mate	20
Edwd. Berry	279
Capt. Saml. Barry	400
Major Wm. Beeston	878
Titus Bowman	78
Jno. Browning	22
Widdow Blackhouse	28
Jas. Barry	27
James Boney	50
More	12
William Bent	110
George Bennet	234
Nicholas Bullis and mate	34
John Baugh	11
Francis Bussell and Smith	60
Henry Bowen and mate	84
Thomas Buttler	31
Phillip Botterill	22
Henry Banfield	20
Jno. Burdis and mate	23
Willm. Bent & Henry Bonner	800
George Blewdall	15
John Belfield	69
Jasper Blanch	6
Jno. Cooper	562
Saml, Conyers	216
Thomas Cater	100
Matt Cotton	40½

	acres.
Joseph Casteele	217½
Richard Collinwood	50
Anciell Cole	20
Jno. Cooke	107
Capt. Thomas Clarke	605
Jno. Cope and Westbury	22
Markham Clouds	7½
Anthony Collier	44
Thomas Burser	211
Jno. Cahaune and mate	11
George Campe	91
William Capon	6
Jno. Clave	20
Edwd. de la Cuz	660
Wm. Davison	240
Nicholas de la Roch	6
Richard Dun	60
Heny Dawkins	15
Robert Davis and Morgan	200
Francis Daniel	33½
Edwd. Exceceune	17
Jno. Edwards and mate	56
Geo. Eccleston	14
William Elder	96
Thomas Edmond	70
Richard Fielder	100
Jeremiah Fowler	63
Morris Fleyne	42
Henry Ford	100
Thomas Flood	3
Wm. Ford	210
Jenkyn Loyd	7
Mary Fisher	7½
William Groves	15
Luke Groce	28
Chas. Griffin	9
James Grimes	7½

	acres.
Sampson George	40
Robert Galloway	9¾
Widdow Gay	74
Jno. Garret	8½
Danl. Garvin	2½
Nathaniel Guy	190
Morgan Hopkins	19
Wm. Hazard	11
Chas. Hudson	44
Lieut. Coll Richd. Hope & ye inhabts ...	970
Lieut. Coll Richd. Hope	1497
Gawen Hill	80
James Howell	1233
Richard Huffelt	8
James Hunt	8
Jno. Hardy	47
Nicholas Hancock	50
Jno. Hone	21
Hest Hammot	6
Gregory Hubbart	48
Geo. Hame	218
Francis Hope	12
Jno. Hattewell	20
William James	60
Walter Jenkins	34
Jno. Johnson	12
Andrew Jewett	30
Jno Jefferies	24
Thomas Joyce	30
Samuel Kearnor	30
Matt Knight	12
Abraham Keeling	60
Wm. Kilgress	8
Wm. Cane	13
Nicholas Keine	643
Jane Leader	19
Widdow Lane	5

	acres.
Francis Lawn	48
Jno Lewis	600
Nicholas LeFord	40
Jacob Lucy and compt.	34
Wm. Lance	336
Jno Maverley	130
Wm. Mayo	40
Sir James Modyford	530
James Manenson	34
Own Macarta	56
Alexander Miles	41
Jno. Murron	14
Christopher Mayan	30
Robt Moody	50
Richd. Mapely	28
William Parker	10
Wm. St. Oniyon	10
Jno. Priest	80½
Jno. Pond	6
Jas. Pinnock	802
Jno. Potter	142½
Joseph Phyfies	84
Jno. Pitts	7½
Jno. Pearse	30
Capt. Wm. Parker	1534
Robt. Pyatt	62
Capt. Wm. Rivers	60
Ralph Rippon	20
John Robinson	46
James Russell	9
Francis Russell and mate	53
Moses Raco	18
Francis Scarlett Esqr.	1000
Edward Stanton and Henry Bonner	500
Edward Manton	374
John Spread	9½

	acres.
Lieut. Jno. Stanley	90
Morris Sheham	4
David Spence	7½
John Stiles and mate	67
Cornelius Struys	122
Thomas South	60
Richard Lemard	7
Jno. Stephens	20
Wm. Sparkes	75
Saml. Sawyer	14
Richard Smith	16
Thos. Sampson	120
Jas. Thompson	18
Thos. Todd and Mate	49
Peter Tarragon	16
Ann Thorne	156
William Tanton	24
Thos. Trinade	38
Peter Turpin	622
Thomas Tattle	40
Wm. Turrill	15
Thos. Tothill	1300
Richd. Teage	88
Capt. Wm. Vallet	220
Thos. Vaughan	37
Richard Wilson	54
William Waters	8
Capt. Samuel Warrner	60
Jno. Williams	30
William Warrington	270
Thos. Taylor	18
Richard Thorne	16
Willm Wilson	80
Hugh Weekes	44
Charles Whitfield	950
Wm. Warren	707
Edwd. Wooden	7½
Thos. Watson	9
Richd. Wood	70

		acres.
Jno. Wilson	... ...	20
Anthy. Woodhouse	... ...	4
George Wattle	... ...	56
Jas. Woodall	... ...	8½
Richd. Valley	... ...	200
Jno. Walker	... ...	308
Charles Whitefield	... ...	51
Henry Wastell and Mate	... ...	16
In this Parish are Families	194	
People by estimation	1552	

ST. CATHERINE'S PARISH.

Jno. Arden	... ...	560
Capt. Richd. Bourden	... ...	2250
Richd. Beckford	... ...	578
Jno. Bonner	... ...	82
William Bunn and mate	... ...	64
Robt. Bedford	... ...	30
Jno. Berry	... ...	40
Lieut. Coll. Robt. Bindloss	... ...	1935
Edward Blackman	... ...	62
Coll. Thomas Ballard	... ...	2391
More	... ...	1000
Peter Burton	... ...	18
Richard Boyne	... ...	148
Susannah Barker	... ...	160
Anthony Burroughs	... ...	40
Thomas Buxden	... ...	67
Francis Barnes	... ...	60
Henry Barrett	... ...	32½
William Burton	... ...	44
Edward Bent	... ...	27
Christopher Buttler	... ...	9
Nicholas Collins	... ...	60
Jno. Casteele	... ...	210
Jno. Collet	... ...	120
Jno. Colebeck	... ...	812
Captain Colebeck and Inhabitants	...	1340
Joshua Cooper	... .	60

	acres
William Cussan	551
Jno. Cater	252
James Casement	190
James Crookshank	90
Matthew Crew	800
Thomas Cox	300
Bryan Clacky	110
Derby Cecil	110
Francis Crookshanke	40
Major Anthony Collier and mates	2600
Coll John Cope	144
Jno Doughty a mate	80
Thomas Davis	440
Wm. Dean	597
Geo. Dawkins and mate	60
Timothy Dodd	300
Oliver Dust	60
Jno. Drinkwater	27
Jno. Ellis	150
Heny Edey	30
George Elkin	3286
Dorothy Eaton	220
Augustine Evans	401
Capt. William Freeman	40
Bartholemew Fant	1430
Angelina Fant	210
William Floyd	60
Widdow Farefield	385
Major Thomas Fuller	1309
Humphrey Freeman Esqr.	627
Tobias Foot	120
Roger Fugas	30
Jno. Fleming	34
Robert Ford	100
Jno. Gimball	618
Andrew Groves	38

	acres.
William Gray	720
Jno. Gillingham	120
Wm. Gibson	45
Richard Guy	270
Joachim Hare	420
William Hebb Esqr.	437
Henry Hilliard	100
Wm. Hill and mate	190
Nicholas Horner	100
Wm. Hubblehouse and mate	160
Anthony Hopper	70
Geo. Hollamfield	140
Geo. Hanboran	450
Edward Hans and mate	123
Richard Hemings	1600
Jno. Halkins and mate	1190
William Herbert	120
Jno. Hillier and Perrat	320
Francis Hall	100
Alice Howell	15
Wm. Harker	164
George Holyday	133
Simon Huse	3
Cary Hellgar	146
Wm. Hobbleton	120
Francis Innians	453
Jno. Jackson	30
William Knowles	760
George Knight	63
Thomas Lyon	96
Samuel Long	18
Thos. Lilly	782
Samuel Lewis and Francis Mann	1555
William Williams Esqr.	522
Capt. Hender Molesworth	2480
Wm. Matthews	520
Jno. Morse	19
Charles Morgan	910

		acres.
Wm. Moseley	... ...	1242
William Morris	... .	40
Bryan Mache	... ...	30
Thomas Modyford Esq. & Co.	... ...	6090
Philip Masters	... ...	411½
Thomas Martin	... ...	130
Hugh Mighty	... ...	140
Wm. Matthews	... ...	170
Sir Jams. Modyford	... ...	3500
Wm. Markham	... ...	33
Lucas Martin	... ...	30
Sir Thos. Modyford	... ...	109
Geo. Menell	... ...	475
George Needham Esq.	... ...	1764
Capt. John Noyes	... ...	5868
William Oaks	... ...	19
John Parson and Mate	... ...	30
Joseph Peters	... ...	30
Francis Phillips	... ...	33
Alexander Pits and mate	... ...	90
Francis Price and mate	... ...	15
Thomas Parnell	... ...	120
Wm. Perkins	... ...	188
Thos. Pitts	... ...	500
Jas. Parsons	... ...	34
Jno. Parish	... ...	175
More	... ...	120
Joseph Peters	... ...	55
George Reekstead	... ...	60
Geo. Russell	... ...	160
Bartholemew Roe	... ...	33
Evan Rice	... ...	120
Jno. Ricgway	... ...	340
Royal Company	... ...	470
Henry Rimes	... ...	530
Thos. Raby	... ...	398
Fulke Rose	... ...	380

	acres.
Jno. Chas. Stevenson	30
John Sticker	90
James Sharpington	60
Henry Saw	400
Geo. Tirton	42
Jno. Thomas and mate	153
Thomas Tyler	210
John Vine	45
Henry Veasy	90
More	33
Thomas Webb	250
Richard Whaley and mate	163
Henry Weston	61
John Went	81½
More	150
John Welling	150
Robert Willias and mate	120
John Wooley and mate	201
George Woodger and Parris	100
Isaac Wells	9
Wm. White	15½
Jno. Whiting	30

In this Parish Families 158
People by estimation 2370

ST. JOHN PARISH.

	acres.
Captain Whitigift Aylmer	294
Major Thomas Ascough	880
William Aldridge and Mate	60
Edward Allen	155
Edw. Arthur	250
Robert Bennett	30
Thos. Burgan	62
Jno. Bagnall	36
Francis Bostock	8¼
Stephen Basnett	276
Edw. Banfield and Mate	100

	acres.
Charles Buckley and mate	205
Wm. Bragg	950
Thos. Bland	8
Henry Barret	300
Thos. Buttler	510
Elizabeth Bagnol	7
Lieut. Col. Jno. Cope	683
Lawrence Charnock & mate	740
Gilbert Cope	80
Robert Cole and mate	23
Jno. Cantrill	21
Nicholas Clarke	210
Jonathan Cock	1000
William Collier	120
Theo. Carey	83
Timothy Dodd	108
Jno. Davis and mate	119
Jno. Davenport Esq.	220
Bartholemew Douse	10
Lieut. John Dowler	9
Robert Evans	18
John Frizell	300
John Frizel and mate	300
Captain Richard Guy	753
William Gaywood	64
Thomas Griffin and mate	171
Richard Garland and mate	60
Joseph Gunn	90
Wm. Gillman	43
Lt. Richard Hysam	90¼
Daniel Harris	7½
Robt. Hazell	270
Thos. Jones	373
Richard Jenkin	108
To the inhabitants of the parish	500
Thomas Johnson	250
Doctor Thos. Jones	20

		acres.
Robt. Kelly	...	300
Capt. Jno. Laugher	...	204
Owen Mason	...	150
Sir Jas. Modyford	...	1000
Capt. Robt. Nelson	...	1300
Captain Richard Oldfeld	...	370
Adrian Peterson	...	250
Francis Price	...	175
Thomas Perry	...	180
Robt. Paine	...	4
Francis Palmer	...	200
Edmund Roe	...	215
Elizt Reid	...	927
Capt. Geo. Reid	...	1403
Edward Rawlins	...	120
Roger Reynolds	...	4
Jno. Steele and mate	...	300
Thomas Small	...	15
Edward Sykes	...	150
Jno. Styles	...	3200
William Sams	...	400
Jno. Stubbs	...	320
Wm. Thorpe	...	68
James Tuckery and mate	...	150
Jno. Trigg	...	90
Richard Vildy	...	60
Jno. Wilson and mate	...	200
Ellis Ward and mates	...	233
Wm. Wright & Co.,	...	418
Saml. Warren	...	360
Edmund Willet	...	72
Jno. White	...	259

In this Parish
Families 83
People by estimation 996

CLARENDON PARISH.

Lewis Anderson	...	58
Jno. Ashley	...	156
Thos. Widden Allwinckle	...	600

	acres.
Cornelius Adams	50
Eleanor Barrett	55
Richard Barrett	149
Jno. Butcher and mates	297½
Geo. Booth	1200
Robert Bariff	100
Widow Bolton	100
Robt. Brownlow	190
Edward Branfield	100
Jno. Baukes and Sheet	60
Ezrael Baldwin	400
Nicholas Bolton	500
Anthony Boroughs	30
Peter Beckford	2238
Lieut. Col. Robt. Bindlos	250
Edward Bull	61
Joseph Bathurst	1200
Major Anthony Collier	1261
Jane Clarke	240
Thos. Caswell	270
Richard Carr	30
Edmund Cross	90
William Courtman	65
Thomas Cole	136
Wm. Coxhead	54
Geo. Child	120
Edwd. Cock	136
Lord Clarendon	3000
Barbara Call	70
Peter Cockup	60
Robert Cooper	90
Capt. Edward Collier	1020
Peter Copacke	160
Henry Dunnett	30
Geo. Downer	210
Jno. Durant	432
Heny Douche	20
Henry Davis	411½

	acres.
Jno. Fisher	138
William Frog	90
William Frame	120
Wm. Follar	30
Hugh Gilbert	93¾
Joseph Gardner	570
Richard Gray	180
William Gent	240
Michael Garrett	91
James Griffin	60
Edward Garrett and mate	30
Richard Green	260
Edward Gerrard	25
Hugh Ginge	20
Jno. Gage	10
Martin Goldin	20
Wm. Gunter	200
Capt. Christopher Horner	1083
Jno. Hill	275
Henry Hilliard	1668
Jno. Hewitt	980
Geo. Holsworth	186
Geo. Hammond	65
Jno. Hunt	120
Richard Hooton and Gunter	100
Richard Haynes	100
Thomas Halse	466
Capt. Joachim Hane	1500
Harman Jacob	305
Lieut. Col. William Ivy	1075
John Jonson	220
Edward Isles	30
Ralph Johnson	40
Ruth Kilby	90
Hugh Hinn	81
Wm. Lord	435
Jno. Loch	35
Robert Little	106

	acres.
Capt. Samuel Long	2200
Jane Lumbard	150
Robert Leeward	100
Jno. Loyd and Frankling	379
Jno. Long	50
Original Lewis	70
Richard May and mates	770
Jno. Marshall	186
Jno. Magill and mate	60
Adair More	90
Jno. Morant	30
Valentine Mamby	105
Francis Man	285
William Mason	185
Richard Masey	50
Daniel Morris	30
Widdow Netherland	120
Jno. Newman	112
Richard Ollife	66
Richard Phelps	320
Jasper Pickerine	550
John Powell	60
Roger Phypes	80
Wm. Pritchett	30
Geo. Pattison	122
Wm. Pearse	42
Ralph Rippon	140
George Ricketts	40
Edward Ray and mate	109
Thomas Roden	243
Edward Rule and mate	330
Philip Roberts	403
Roger Ramsay & mate	41½
Thos. Robinson & Mate	50
George Ragg	36
Elias Sedgwick	10
Francis Starkey	227
Francis Sperry	349
More	240

		acres.
Jno. Smith	... ...	76
Robt. Smith	... ...	180
Robt. Stone	... ...	75
Jno. Stiles	... ...	90
Jno. Sherwin	... ...	30
Nathaniel Shin and mate	... ...	84
Robert Smart	... ...	60
Michael Sanders	... .	120
Jno. Shaw	... ...	450
Amos Stevens	... ...	10
Jno. Sheppard	... ...	185
Jno. Skelling	... ...	210
Jno. Thompson	... ...	300
Joseph Taylor	... ...	12
Jno. Taylor	... ...	190
Jno. Townshend	... ...	210
Benjamin Tillingham	... ...	300
Robt. Varney Esquire	... ...	701
Jno. Vizard	... ...	120
Priscilla Willoughby	... ...	600
Jno. Warren	... ...	188
Robt. Warner and mate	... ...	350
Robt. Wright	... ...	100
Tobias Winsor	... ...	60
Thos. Waite	... ...	88
Thos. Wiles	... ...	32
In this Parish are Families	143	
People by estimation	1430	

An abstract of the whole Parishes

	acres patented	Families	Numbers of persons
St. Thomas Parish	14825½	59	590
St. Davids Parish	11946¾	80	960
St. Andrews Parish	29199¾	194	1552
St. Catherines Parish	68590	158	2374
St. Johns Parish	25197¾	83	996
Clarendon Parish	39260¾	143	1430

NOTE.—Privateers Hunters Sloop and Boatmen as at   2500

We likewise calculate the privateers Hunters Sloop and boats many which ply about the Island and are not reckoned in any of the above parishes to be at least 2500 able lusty men. The four Parishes on the Northside viz St. Georges, St, M‿rys, St. Anne's and St. James and the leeward most Parish St. Elizabeth hath not been yet collected as not worth it, by

    reason of its distance
    and new settlements where
    we find about 20000 acres patented
    and calculate there cannot be
    less than 1500 people   20000   1500

                        209020½ 717 11898

    More we calculate of persons
    in the towns of Port Royal and St.
    Jago to be no less than men women
    and children   3300

                        15198

The Receiver General hath not received any rent these two years it not being worth the going so far for every year, the last collection amounting to but £151 9/- whereof some being for 3 and some two years But now this Michaelmas he begins to collect for 2 years and is ordered at the same time to take an exact account of all the persons in every Family, which with the Rentall (when finished) shall be presented for His Majestys view, and we are confident will amount to one half more at least than the above calculation this being guessed at according to the last collection made 2 years since.

Commodities which this Island produceth with a calculation of the Quantities of some of them—

Here are 57 Sugar Works which may produce yearly 1710 thousand weight of sugar, those still increasing, and others a going up.

Also 47 Cocoa Walks which may yield 188000 pound weight of nuts in seasonable years, these improving, and many young walks planted, which will very speedily produce.

Also 49 Indigo works which may produce about 49000 weight of Indigo p. annum, to which many more works are daily adding.

Three salt Ponds containing 4000 and odd acres under the management of Capt. Noge yielded this year about 10000

Bushels he affirming to have been able to make as many tuns, if he could have had vent for it.

The Mountains are full of Pumento also Jamaica Pepper everywhere, and some have planted it, so that if there were encouragement there might be yearly sent of about 50000 weight.

Here is also an undestroyable quantity of Fustick, Brasiletto, Lignum Votae, Ebony, sweet smelling and other curious woods for several uses of which great quantities are daily exported.

We have also Anotto by the Spaniard called Acheot began to be made which we expect will prove a great commodity.

WE have also Vanillious, China Roots, Cassia Fistula and Tamarinds, which the Planters do endeavonr to encrease they being very good Drugs.

We find the land very good for cotton and Tobacco but the other Commodities being more staple and profitable very few busy themselves with it—

We have large Savannas, and now great stocks of Cattle which we judge have increased within these six years from 60 tame cattle to 6000.

Sheep goats and tame Hogs great Plenty, so that we are past all Danger of Want, and hope in a short time to be able to furnish the ships homewards bound.

By His Excellencys Command

    sgd.   Thos. Tothill

                Receiver General.

PART IX.

PEDIGREE OF ROBERT HUNTER GOVERNOR OF JAMAICA.

PEDIGREE OF MAJOR GENERAL ROBERT HUNTER.
GOVERNOR OF JAMAICA 1727-8—1734.

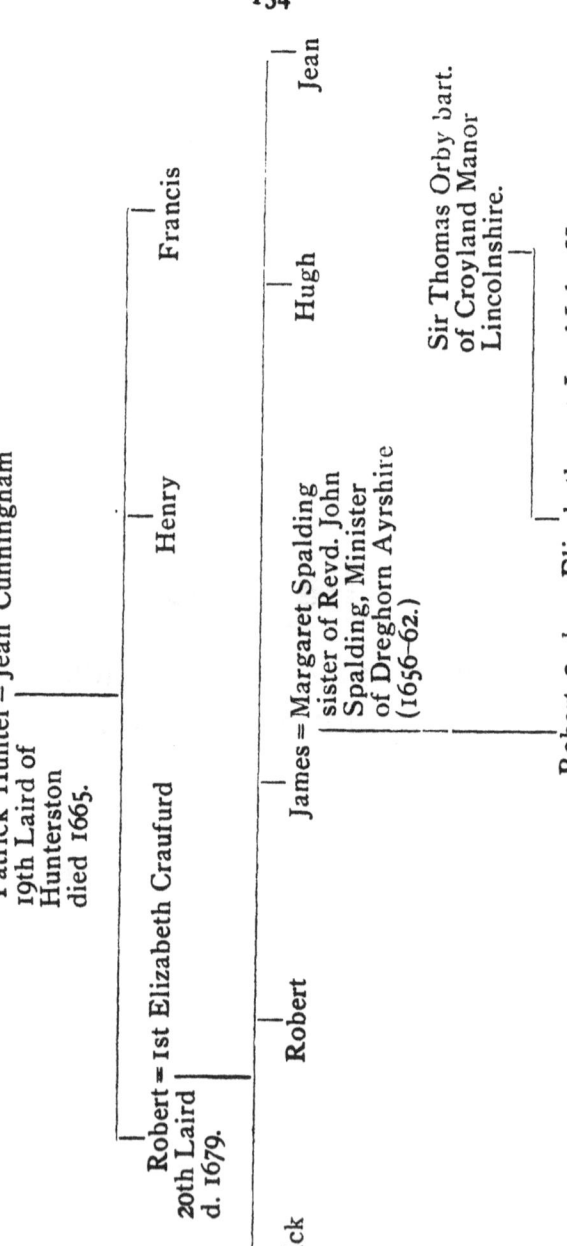

Robert Hunter (Governor of Jamaica) saw much active service, having fought with Ross's Dragoons at the battle of Blenheim in 1704.

He was appointed Governor of Virginia but on his way to assume that position in 1708 he was captured by the French and taken back to Europe, being shortly afterwards exchanged for the French Bishop of Quebec, an English prisoner. In 1707 he was appointed by Queen Anne "Captain General and Governor-in-Chief in and over Her Majesty's Provinces of New York and New Jersey and Territories depending thereon in America and Vice Admiral of the same." He held this position for nine years and on retiring was presented with an address by the Assembly and is described by American writers "as a man of good temper and discernment, the best and ablest of the Royal Governors of New York."

On the death of the Duke of Portland (1726) Hunter was appointed to succeed him as Governor of Jamaica where he died 31st March 1734—there was according to the Rev. John Nichols in his Literary Anecdotes of the 18th Century (Vol. VI. p.p. 89 and 90) a long latin inscription placed on his tomb; I am however unaware of the present existence of this tomb.

General Hunter left one son and three daughters—his great grandson Thomas Orby Hunter was the last of his male descendants, he left however three daughters the youngest of whom married in 1824 Sir George Wombwell (third baronet) of Wombwell, Yorkshire.

(I am indebted for most of the foregoing to Andrew A. Hunter Esq. of The College, Cheltenham.)

ADDENDA.

NOTE 1. INTRODUCTION.

The following additional information as to some of the Parishes of Jamaica may be useful.

PORT ROYAL.	Incorporated with the Parish of Saint Andrew in 1867.
SAINT DAVID.	Incorporated with the Parish of Saint Thomas in the East in 1867.
PORTLAND.	Originally a part of Saint Thomas in the East made a parish in 1723 and named after the Duke of Portland then Governor.
SAINT GEORGE.	Incorporated with Portland in 1867.
MANCHESTER.	Made a Parish in 1814 from the adjoining Parishes of Saint Elizabeth and Clarendon and named after William Duke of Manchester the then Governor.
SAINT JOHN. SAINT DOROTHY. SAINT THOMAS IN THE VALE.	Incorporated with Saint Catherine in 1867.
METCALFE.	Created a Parish in 1842 and named after Governor Sir Charles Theophilus Metcalfe. Incorporated with Saint Mary in 1867.
WESTMORELAND.	Created a Parish in 1703 being separated from the Parish of Saint Elizabeth.
TRELAWNEY.	Created a Parish in 1774 being a portion of the Parish of Saint James.
VERE.	Incorporated with Clarendon in 1867.
HANOVER.	Created in 1723 out of the Parish of Westmoreland.

NOTE 2. PAGE 41.

Copy of Entries in old Prayer Book—dated 1770—belonging to Elizabeth H. Price Febry. 2nd 1771 and then to John Hudson Guy 1795 (now in possession of MRS. W. E. M. DRUMMOND—Jamaica).

ENTRIES IN VARIOUS HANDWRITINGS.

"On Saturday May 21st 1737 Elizabeth Hannah Guy daughter of John Hudson Guy and Elizabeth his wife was born at Donnington Castle near the town of Newbury in the County of Berkshire. They all arrived in Jamaica June 1742.

On Wednesday Febry. 7th John Hudson Guy died aged 52 in the year 1749–50. Born the 23rd May 1698.

On Sunday Febry. 24th 1750–51 Eliza Hannah Guy was married to John Woodcock.

On Sunday August 18th 1754 Eliza Guy died aged 49.

On Wednesday night 12 o'clock Decr. 17th 1755 Edward Young Woodcock son of John Woodcock and Elizabeth Hannah his wife was Born at Berkshire Hall Estate in the Parish of St. Thomas in the Vale.

Edward Young Woodcock went to England in June 1763.

Edward Young Woodcock son of Jas. and Eliz H. Woodcock died in Span Town December 1749 Æ 39 nearly would have been on 17 Dec.

J. H. Guy Esq. formerly Chief Justice born 23rd May 1698 Obt. 7 Febry. 1750 Æ 52.

His son J. H. Guy born 29 June 1727 Obt. 4 June 1761 Æ 34.

His son born 27 Jany. 1754 J. H. Guy and Millicent his wife born 18 Febry. 1761.

Their son John Hudson Guy born 31 Octr. 1787—Millicent Guy born 15 Decr. 1788—Sarah Guy born 19 February 1791—Edward Freeman Guy born 26th August 1793—Mary Ann Guy born 27th July 1797.

My dear daughter Millicent Guy was married to James Seton Lane Esq. at Hayfield 30th September 1809 Millicent Lane their daughter born at Cool Shade 3rd July 1810 their son James Lane born at Cool Shade 21st October Obt. 3 in the morning 1811. My dear daughter Sarah Guy was married to George Barriffe 21st December 1811 at Hayfield. John Hudson Guy Esq. age 63 died 11th (day) of August between 1-2 o'clock 1816.

On Monday Septr. 1768 John Woodcock died at his estate Donnington Castle in the Parish of St. Mary.

On Tuesday Octr. 4th 1768 Elizabeth Hannah Woodcock was married to Charles Price Esq. son of Sir Charles Price Bart. and Mary his wife born in Kingston Novr. 26th 1732 he arrived in Jamaica the end of Novr. 1753.

Elizabeth Hannah Price died 5 July 1771 Æ 34.

Sir Charles Price Bart. her husband died 18th Octr. 1788 Æ 56.

Lady Lydia Ann Price his last wife died 6th Nov. 1795 Æ 55.

Mary Ann Guy married to James Forsyth Esqr. 8th October 1817 at Hayfield St. Thomas in the Vale by the Revd. Mr. Burton.

Mrs. Mary Eccles died October 31st 1821.

Mrs. Margaret P. Bicknell died July 12th 1821. Henry P. Bicknell died Augt. 8 1827.

Millicent Lane died the 15th of July 1840. Her daughter Millicent Williamson died the 19th of October 1839.

My beloved Mother Millicent Fletcher Guy died at Hayfield Pen St. Thomas in the Vale on the 7 of December 1843 aged 82 years. Buried at the Parish Church on the 2nd Decr. 1843.

Mrs. Sarah Bariffe died 2nd Janry. 1867."

INDEX.

NOTE.—The List of Inhabitants commencing on page III are not indexed as it is alphabetically arranged (initial letter) under each Parish.

A.

	PAGE.	
Aberdeen	37	
Addenbrook	43	
Addenda	137	
Alexander	98	
Allen	11	45
Allen vs. Pennington	11	
Arcedeckne	21	
Armstrong	12	
Armstrong vs. Gordon	12	
Ashburne	70	
Ashley	13	72
Ashley vs. Dawkins	13	
Atkins	98	
Audley	14	
Audley vs. O'Brien	14	
Aylmer	15	
Aylmer vs. Alymer	15	
Aylemore	97	
Ayscough	32	100

B.

	PAGE.	
Ballard	100	
Barbados	64	
Barclay	37	
Barn	26	
Barrett	46	
Barritt	16	19
Barry	100	
Barton	43	
Basnett	17	78
Basnett vs. Garthwaite	17	
Batchelor	65	
Bates	33	
Bathurst	15	
Beckford	43	
Beckett	67	
Beeston	99	
Berkshire	43	
Blackheath	42	
Blair	67	
Blake	18	
Blake vs. Crowder	18	
Bonner	12	72
Booth	19	
Bosley	20	
Bosley vs. Wheatle	20	
Bourden	97	
Bowen	46	
Brailsford	78	
Brayne	31	
Brissett	44	46
Brodbelt	73	
Brooks	26	
Brown	42	

	PAGE.	
Browne	15	98
Bryden	51	
Buchanan	13	
Bunbury	42	
Burke	15	21
Burke vs. Hall	21	
Butt	55	
Byndloss	22	99
Byndloss vs. Martins	22	

C.

	PAGE.				
Callendar	39				
Campbell	61				
Cappogwin	26				
Carberry (Earl of)	80				
Carhampton (Earl of)	47				
Chambers	46				
Chard	49				
Charlestown	57				
Charron	11				
Chidley	58				
Chislet	58				
Chovett	23				
Chovett vs. Arcedeckne	23				
Clarke	39	42	46	64	78
Connor	26				
Connor vs. Brooks	26				
Collier	98				
Cope	97				
Cook	17				
Cooper	100				
Cork	49	56			
Corr	12				
Crawford	134				
Crichton	24				
Crighton vs. Hall	24				
Croasdale	25				
Croasdale vs. Bayley	25				
Croft	62				
Cuddon	57				
Cunningham	134				

D.

	PAGE.
Darwent	65
Darwent vs. Higgins	65
Davenport	29
Dawes	28
Dawkins	27
Dawkins vs. Young	27
Dehany	46
Derbyshire	65
Dorrill	61
Douglas	28
Douglas vs. Dawes	28
Dowlen	29

INDEX.

D.	PAGE.	H.	PAGE.
Dowlen vs. Freeman	29	Halstead	44
Downer	33	Halstead vs. Brown	15 44
Downer vs. Reid	30	Hanover Square	46
Drax	31	Hanses	45
Drax vs. Brayne	31	Hanses vs. Campbell	45
D'Warris	55	Hargreaves	25
E.		Haughton	46 54
East	24	Haughton vs. Haughton	46
Edgegoose	99	Hay, Lord	134
Edlyne	68	Hervey	43
Edinburgh	37	Heylin	78
Elletson	68 75	Higgins	65
Elletson vs. Taylor	75	Hill	57 72
Ellis	43	Hilton	42
Elmers	78	Holley	98
Etough	25	Holsworth	40
F.		Home (Countess of) vs. Home (Earl of)	} 47
Fay	14		
Fearon	21	Home (Dowager Countess of) vs. Luttrell	} 47
Fleming	69		
Ford	32	Home, Earl of	47
Ford vs. Mitchell	32	Hope	99
Forres	71	Horner	98
Forster	21	Hughes	48
Freeman	29 63 98	Hughes vs. Powell	48
Freeman vs. Bennett	33	Humphrey	78
Freeman vs. Putman	33	Hunter	134
Fuller	97	**I.**	
Furnell	23	Inhabitants	111
G.		Ireland	15 21 26 49 56
Gardner	34	Irnham Lord	47
Gardner vs. Beckford	84	Ivy	98
Gibbons	47	**J.**	
Gill	64	Jenkes	100
Gillespie	36	Jenning	41
Gillespie vs. Hume	36	Jessop	49
Gibraltar	47	Jessop vs. Johnson	49
Glocester	65	Johnson	35 49
Goodwin	30	Jones	58
Gordon	37 38	Jowett	25
Gordon vs. Cargill	37	**K.**	
Gordon vs. MacKay	38	Keene	99
Grabham	58	Kelly	26
Grace	39	Kent	42
Grace vs. Clarke	39	King	50
Graham	53 75	King vs. Pasco	50
Great Britain	32 40 42	**L.**	
Green Dragoons	26	Lambeth (South)	20
Grifin	36	Lamond vs. Jackson	51
Griffith	56	Langley	97
Guthrie vs. Scott	40	Lawrence	26
Guy	23 29 41	Lawrence vs. Witter	52
Guy vs. Jennings	41	Laws	47
H.		Lenderson	58
Haden	42	Lincoln	134
Haden vs. Clarke	42	Lincoln Inn	48
Halhed vs. Barton	43	List of Inhabitants	111
Hall	42 78	Litchfield	46

INDEX.

L.

	PAGE.
Litteljohn	33
Litteljohn vs. Cargill	53
Livingston	26
Lloyd	29 100
Loakes	57
London	57 72
Long	23 43 98
Luttrell	47
Luttrell vs. Earl of Carhampton	47

M.

	PAGE.
Macey	79
MacKay	38
MacKenzie	54
MacKie	71
MacLean	55
Malcolm	54
Malcolm vs. MacKenzie	54
Mann vs. D'Warris	55
Mansfield	26
Masters	57
Maverly	23
Mayo Viscount	15
Mee	56
Mee vs. Blair	55
Mercers Chappell	65
Merida	36
Middlesex	48
Millward vs. Bayley	57
Mingham	62
Mitchell	32
Mogridge	58
Mogridge vs Laws	58
Montego Bay	60
Moore	59 60
Moore vs. Fenton	59
Morton	51
Moseley	97
Mumbee	27
Mure vs. Senior	61
Murray	71
Musgrave	58

N.

	PAGE.
Newcastle	26
New Jersey	11
New York	40
Nicholls	62
Nicholls vs. Waight	62
Northbury	58
Northumberland	51
Noy	63
Nuttall	40

O.

	PAGE.
Oldfield	97
Oliver	113
Orby	134
Ord	75
Osborn	63
Osborn vs. Freeman	63
Owen	78

P.

	PAGE.
Pallmer	21 43
Parker	14 43 98
Pasco	50
Patterson	46
Pawlett (Lord)	80
Peace	99
Pearce	58
Pennant	100
Perry	64
Perry vs. Bernard	64
Perse	65
Perse vs. Batchelor	65
Philp	24 66
Philp vs. Pusey	66
Phipps	67
Phipps vs. Williams	67
Piccadilly	62
Pilminster	58
Pommells	26
Powell	48
Putman } Putnam }	35
Pusey	66

Q.

	PAGE.
Quarrell	28

R.

	PAGE.
Reid	30
Richardson	68
Richardson vs. Beckford	68
Riddock	69
Riddock vs. Fleming	69
Rio Bueno	69
Rippon	70
Rippon vs. Whincop	70
Roberts	79
Robertson	71
Robertson vs. Forbes	71
Robinson	42
Rookwood	24
Rosewell	56
Rule	13
Russell	14 72
Russell vs. Bonner	72

S.

	PAGE.
Saint George	46
Saint Mary Ax	72
Salton Lord	37
Scotland	71
Senior	61
Sergeant	78
Sinclair	38
Slape	58
Somerset	11 58
South Carolina	57
Southy	58

INDEX

S.	PAGE.	V.	PAGE.
Spalding	134	Vassall	61 76
Staffold	72	*Vassall vs. Stout*	76
Stewart vs. Brodbelt	73	Vaughan (Lord)	80
Stout	76	**W,**	
Surrey	20	Wallace	61
Survey (list of Inhabitants)	111	Wales	48
Sutton	74	Wallin	77
Sutton vs. Moore	74	Waite	62
Swanton	49	Waller	46
Swanzy (Swansea)	48	Walrond	97
Sympson	22	Warner	99
T.		Warren	73
Tate	51 69	Waterford	26
Taunton	58	Westhorpe	40
Taunton St. Mary		White	61
Magdalen	58	Whitfield	99
Taunton St. James	58	Wignal	73
Taylor	46 75	*Wignal vs. Hall*	78
Taylor vs. Gregory	75	Wilkins	79
Taylor vs. Haughton	46	*Wilkins vs. Gale*	79
Terrick	46	Williams	52
Tharpe	46	*Winchester Marquis of vs. Heywood*	80
Thompson	37		
Tinley	69	Wilton	58
Tinling	51	Winiot	58
Tipperary	26	Witherington	45
Totterdell	29	Witter	28
Townsend	67	Wood	23 46 65
Trowers	77	Wyett	78
Trull	58	**Y.**	
Turpin	33	Yeamans	67
V.		Yeeles	61
Vallett	99	Young	37

www.ingramcontent.com/pod-product-compliance
Lightning Source LLC
Chambersburg PA
CBHW051944160426
43198CB00013B/2286